Seaside School

The Story of the Hornsea Centre
1938 - 1998

John McLeod

Yorkshire Art Circus

Published 1999 by **Yorkshire Art Circus**
School Lane, Glasshoughton, Castleford, WF10 4QH
Tel: 01977 550401
Fax: 01977 512819
e-mail: books@artcircus.org.uk
www.artcircus.org.uk

© Text: John McLeod

Support: Ian Daley, Lorna Hey, Ian Clayton, Jonathon Bell

Cover Design: Paul Miller of Ergo Design
Printed by FM Repro, Liversedge

ISBN: 1 898311 43 9

British Library Cataloguing in Publication Data.
A catalogue record for this book is available from the British Library.

Yorkshire Art Circus is a unique book publisher. We work to increase access to writing and publishing and to develop new models of practice for arts in the community.
Please write to us for details of our full programme of workshops and our current book list. Our Website is http://www.artcircus.org.uk
Yorkshire Art Circus is a registered charity No 1007443.

Yorkshire Art Circus is supported by:

I very much welcome the publication of this book about the Hornsea Centre. For over 60 years Hornsea has served the children of the City of Wakefield and the wider Metropolitan District and there is every prospect of it continuing to do so for many years into the future. It meets a real need, both socially and educationally. Hornsea's story is a fascinating one: and this book is a significant contribution to Wakefield's social history. I hope that you will enjoy reading it.

Councillor Robert Mitchell

The idea for this book came to me after a visit to the Hornsea Centre with colleagues in June 1996. The Warden produced three log books and suggested that they ought to be preserved in Wakefield for safe keeping. Reading them later that day took me back into an almost forgotten world, quite remote from the one inhabited by Education Officers today : and so the idea of commemorating Hornsea's 60th anniversary was born.

There are many people whose help in making this book possible needs to be acknowledged. Councillor Robert Mitchell, Chair of Wakefield Education Committee, has been unfailingly encouraging. Joanne Tolson's enthusiasm for the project and research skills blazed a trail through the archives for me. The Education Department's typing section typed early drafts from a difficult manuscript, and my Secretary, Mrs Christine Frost, has toiled far beyond the call of duty to produce the final version. I am also grateful to my colleagues in the Education Department who have had to endure tales from Hornsea in and out of season for much of the last few months. They have shown their usual tolerance of their Chief Officer's eccentricities.

Ian Daley and Jo Henderson of Yorkshire Art Circus agreed to publish the book and I am grateful for their help and advice, and for their work in gathering oral reminiscences of some of the older Hornsea 'graduates'.

The staff at the Local History Collection at Balne Lane Library were always helpful and interested, and directed me to material I might not otherwise have seen, and the West Yorkshire Archive Service performed a major feat of detective work by discovering the log book covering the latter half of the 1950s, which had been presumed lost. Phil Atkins of the National Railway Museum found for me some fascinating material on Hornsea in the 1930s. The staff of the Hornsea Centre were kind enough to spend an afternoon with me sharing their memories of children, staff and wardens; unfortunately not all are printable!

Frank Jeffries at the *Wakefield Express* supplied a number of photographs.

I am especially grateful to those people who took the trouble to respond to articles in the *Wakefield Express* seeking memories of visits to Hornsea, and to others who shared memories and impressions of the Seaside School and the Hornsea Centre. They are:

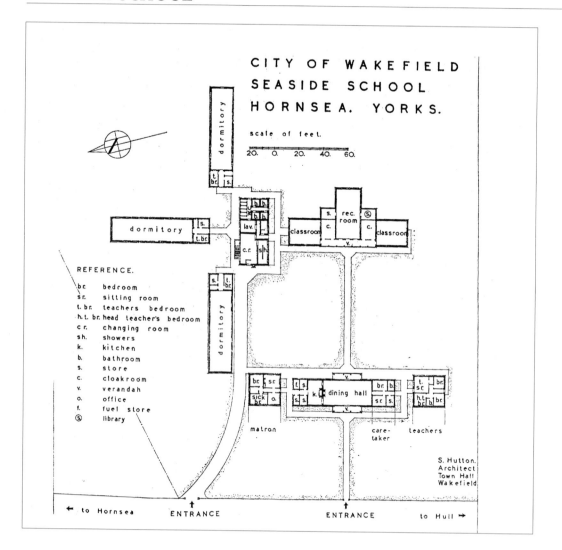

Mrs J. Ambler; Mrs B. Audley; Mr J. Banks; Miss J. L. Batty; Mrs L. Beresford; Joyce Blazek; Mrs F. Bramley; Mr R. Brooke; Mrs G. Burridge; Miss E. Bywater; Mr D. Carr; Miss M. Chapman; Mrs B. Coe; Mr H. Critchlow; Mrs S. Deller; Mrs D. Eccles; Mrs S. Ellis; Mrs D. Gill; Mr B. Greenwood; Mrs P. Haigh; Mr C. Hampson; The late Mr R. Holmes; Mrs E. Heslop; Mr M. Hunt; Mr G. Jackson; Mrs J. Johnson; Mr A. Lancaster; Mr M. Lee; Mrs C. Miller; Mrs M. Milner; Miss L. Mulroy; Mrs S. Parkin; Mrs M. Rayner; Mrs H. Riley; Mrs M. Senior; Mr D. Shaw; Mrs J. Stacey; Miss E. Spurr; Mrs J. Taylor; Mrs J. Tolson; Mrs J. Willey; Mrs J. Wood; and Mrs S. Watson.

I must also thank those teachers of the Wakefield City LEA who conscientiously filled in the log books up to 1974, and who provided much of the source material for this book. Some of the entries are richly entertaining: this book would have been far longer if I had quoted as much as I could have done.

I have become increasingly conscious while writing this account of the Hornsea Centre, of how much the place has meant to so many Wakefield people of an older generation - and of how much it still offers to pupils as we approach the millennium. It is a remarkable survivor. I hope that this book will rekindle some happy memories of the Seaside School and will confirm its place in the history of Wakefield City and district. Hornsea was the product of idealism, on the part of officers and elected members: the sort of idealism difficult to rekindle in the finance-led and target driven education system we have to operate today. Its creation and survival is an important reminder of values we need to retain for the health of local education now and in the future. I have very much enjoyed the task of writing the book (which has dominated my spare time since the beginning of 1998), and I hope that is evident also.

John McLeod
County Hall
May 1999

CHAPTER 1

THIS INTERESTING AND VALUABLE DEVELOPMENT

Wakefield in the 1930s was a small but dynamic local authority. It was a relatively recently created County Borough, having achieved that status in 1915, and, with a population which hovered around 60,000 people, was one of the smallest of its type in the country.

But Wakefield took its responsibilities seriously. It claimed to be 'in the front rank of civic enterprise in the British Isles', and even allowing for a measure of municipal hyperbole, perhaps allowable in a publication called *Wakefield Commercially Considered* in which that claim was made, it is clear that the Council was energetic in promoting the reputation of the city and was willing to undertake major public works which would both encourage investment in Wakefield and improve the lives of its inhabitants.

Wakefield had of course not been immune from the effects of the great depression and world financial crisis of the late 1920s: there was poverty and high unemployment within its boundaries. It was perhaps fortunate in having a rather more diverse economy than other industrial centres. Though mining and textiles were dominant, there was significant employment in the distributive trades and engineering, and as the seat of county government for the West Riding, there was a strong administrative base. Nevertheless, the Council wanted to attract new employers, and was willing to 'sell' the city and create the sort of infrastructure which would make the place attractive to newcomers.

The marketing of Wakefield was perhaps conducted with a degree of advertiser's licence.

In writing his preface to *Wakefield Commercially Considered* the mayor, Alderman Butterworth, could write lyrically and unblushingly:

'Wakefield, in spite of years of industrial prosperity has remained unspoiled. Industry has not soiled our landscape...she has grown up gracefully among her green fields, industry subduing its outward manifestations to the pleasant environment in which it has found itself. She has none of the deep scars that the industrial revolution made in so many English towns'.

Certainly Wakefield's population did not yet sprawl over the surrounding areas to the extent seen in other industrial centres: both industry and people were concentrated along the

Calder and in the old city centre, but successive boundary extensions had incorporated large areas of undeveloped land to the north and west of the city, and in the 1930s the Council was undertaking a remarkably extensive programme of slum clearance and rehousing. By 1936 the Medical Officer of Health was able to report the building of over 3600 Council houses since 1920. "Well housed workers make happy and contented employees" claimed the Council's copywriters. In the mid-1930s, the focus of municipal housing development was on the Lupset area, where nearly 2000 houses were being built. This was a showplace estate, described by the Medical Officer of Health as "a delight to the eye and a credit to the city" : those sentiments were fully shared by other observers, who might have been expected to display more independent judgement.

The *Wakefield Express* article, "In Praise of Lupset", published on 24 August, 1935, is not only a glowing tribute to the new housing development and those who promoted it: it also reflects a high degree of civic pride in what was only one of several major improvements undertaken in the city in the 1930s. Alongside the housing programme, which was a continuing preoccupation, the Council had constructed the modern Chantry Bridge, which had opened in 1933, new sewage treatment works below Primrose Hill, and had improved the water supply by creating the Ryburn reservoir in the distant Pennines. The Council liked to point to progress in other respects, like the closure of the tramway system and its full replacement by motor buses; the relocation of the Municipal Art Gallery to its present home in Wentworth Terrace in 1933 provided the occasion for Councillors to launch a collection focusing on contemporary art, to "keep in touch with modern art in its relations to modern life"; and the city was able to claim, apropos its education system, that "everything is done to help along technical progress ... every possible encouragement is given to ensure an intelligent population that can be further educated for executive positions later on".

The desire to improve standards of public health underpinned much of the Council's thinking. In spite of the clearance programme, there remained much sub-standard and overcrowded housing in the city centre and the "health and safety" controls on industry and commerce were much less stringent than they are today.

Children (and adults) were still at risk from physical illnesses, which are now relatively rare. Between 1931 and 1935, there were over 1400 cases of Scarlet Fever, and in the same period over 1270 cases of Diphtheria were recorded, with 109 deaths (the highest level in the century at that time). Measles could still kill (17 deaths in 1931-35), and so could Whooping Cough (14 deaths). Tuberculosis was still common, especially among older people. Better housing, improved diets and clean water supplies were clearly contributing to improvements in public health. (Enteric Fever, for example, had been eradicated). Child health was improving by the availability of milk, school meals, and an active school health service. However, the Medical Officer of Health was emphatic that more had to be done:

'Public Health practice is no static thing, but presses onwards with something of the restlessness of a mountaineer, whose joy in achievement is but momentary for presently another peak obscures the horizon and must be conquered'.

In spite of the improvement in child health overall, infectious diseases were still affecting school attendance, which struggled to reach 90% overall, and lack of basic health education (or amenities at home) meant that a number of children were allowed to come to school verminous or in "an otherwise dirty condition". In 1938, as many as 178 children were the subject of warning notices in that respect, and in his Annual Report the Director of Education felt it necessary to comment with some severity on the issue:

'In view of the rapid strides which have been made in rehousing and the very extensive and reliable service rendered by the school medical officers and nurses, it is deplorable that any child should be found in such a condition that it is unsafe to allow him or her to remain in contact with others whose parents do all they can to keep their children clean'.

He went so far as to suggest that the magistrates might have to be asked to deal severely with offending parents.

So far as child health was concerned, the Medical Officer of Health, who had a dual role, also serving as Principal School Medical Officer, was convinced of the benefit of Open Air treatment for delicate and "debilitated" children. From just before the First World War there had been growing interest nationally in the possibilities of Open Air Schools. Relatively few purpose-built Open Air schools were ever constructed, though some of their features were incorporated in ordinary elementary schools, and a number of urban authorities, Bradford and Sheffield among them, did pioneering work in promoting the benefits of open air education. Characteristics of Open Air schools in their classic form included a rural site, classrooms which could be opened up on at least one side so that teaching was virtually out of doors, resting sheds and facilities for bathing. Their use was often confined to sickly children and what would now be called a health education curriculum was given some emphasis: at Whiteley Woods School in Sheffield, for example, personal hygiene was taught to all pupils.

The experience of the Open Air schools, and the physical improvement they helped bring about in those who attended, were to have a marked influence on school design. The schools erected following the Education Act of 1870, which introduced universal elementary education, tended to make solid, but rather basic provision, with children confined to classrooms for much of the day, and breaks taken in relatively small, confined quadrangles. The provision of grounds and playing fields was seen as less important than ensuring that sufficient classroom space was available. As the 20th century progressed, a wider view of what schools could do for their children became more prevalent: physical well being was seen as becoming as important as intellectual (and moral) development. In Wakefield, the new thinking was first seen in the design of Manygates School, opened in 1928, which allowed children easy access to the quadrangles via folding and sliding windows, and most especially in the Snapethorpe Schools, developed to serve the expanding Lupset estate, and explicitly designed to be "of the semi open-air type, receiving the maximum of sunlight".

As far as Dr. Allardice, the Medical Officer of Health, was concerned, these developments were insufficient. His report for 1934/35 grumbled that the "School Medical Service of this city still falls short of comprehensiveness in its obligations to the delicate child... the need for an Open Air school is still very apparent to those who are responsible for the medical supervision of the Wakefield schools. Much can be, and is, done in ordinary schools to ensure a maximum of time being spent out of doors in suitable weather, but no amount of resourcefulness can compensate for the lack of a school environment devised to meet special needs."

The school health service tried to compensate for the lack of a fully-fledged open air school in Wakefield by running an Artificial Sunlight Clinic, equipped with a "double suspended Jesionek Mercury Vapour Lamp and a Sollux 1000 watts Radiant Heat Lamp". This treated "debility", whether following cases of Whooping Cough and Measles or associated with nervous symptoms, malnutrition and so on, as well as Rickets, Bronchitis, skin diseases, inflammation of the glands and Tuberculosis. The treatments were of variable efficacy, and the Principal School Medical Officer was not slow to draw attention to cases where open-air school treatment could be beneficial. Even moves to establish the Seaside School at Hornsea, though felt likely to have "a beneficial effect on the school provision generally" had been criticised as still leaving "completely untouched the special facilities necessary for dealing with delicate children". However, Hornsea would be welcomed "with open arms as a material contribution towards raising the general standards of health among school children."

Dr Allardice depended on his colleague, the new Director of Education, to deliver at least in part his vision of a school which would promote children's health. C. L. Berry had been appointed to Wakefield in July 1934, having previously been Director of Education in Todmorden, a "Part III" authority, dealing only with elementary education. In Wakefield, he inherited a system which made very extensive provision.

At the apex of the educational pyramid stood the Queen Elizabeth Grammar School and the Girls' High School, which between them admitted those children from the elementary schools who scored the highest marks in the scholarship examinations, then the two selective schools (for boys and girls) maintained by Wakefield LEA at Thornes House. There was a Technical College, a school of Art and Crafts and a Day Commercial School, a Selective Central School for boys and girls (Ings Road), 38 elementary school departments, five domestic science centres, six woodwork centres, three metal work centres, four junior evening institutes, five women's institutes and three men's institutes.

Wakefield could also claim to be progressive in another respect.

It was one of those authorities which had responded most quickly, and completely, to the Hadow Report of 1926 on *The Education of the Adolescent*. That report had recommended a break at age 11, with children aged 11-14 separated from infants and juniors, and educated in senior schools or divisions. By 1938, some 83% of Wakefield pupils aged 11+ were being educated along Hadow lines. This was the most thoroughgoing reorganisation in West Yorkshire: only Doncaster County Borough came close with 79% of its senior pupils in reorganised classes; the average for England and Wales was 55%. Reorganisations had not taken place in some Church schools, although of those, St Austin's had made distinct arrangements for advanced instruction for older pupils and such changes were being seriously considered elsewhere. In his annual report for 1934/35, Berry could write that 'the City of Wakefield can congratulate itself on having proceeded so far, so successfully and so amicably, with reorganisation'.

The Hadow reorganisation had been accomplished against the background of the national financial crisis referred to above: teachers' salaries had been cut as part of the public expenditure restrictions. The cut was only restored in 1935, and Berry lamented that his budget proposals for that year had been cut by £7419, so that the Education Committee was "still in arrears with important matters such as provision of school accommodation for mentally defective children, of an open air school for physically defective and delicate children, provision for playing fields, bicycle sheds for senior schools, improvements to playgrounds, indoor sanitary provision for infants and other necessary developments."

He had cause to complain, in terms which are not unfamiliar to his successors as Chief Officer in Wakefield, that the authority spent less than the average on elementary education: twelve shillings and five pence less per head than other County Boroughs and sixteen shillings less than the average for all authorities.

Berry's annual reports for the period up to 1938, which cover the period of the planning and opening of the Hornsea Seaside School, have in general an optimistic tone, in spite of the undercurrent of financial concerns. His first report noted that he had seen how 'children love to be at school: that response should stimulate us all to further service on their behalf'.

He was happy to record how closely the LEA worked with the Managers of the Voluntary schools, how there was 'an entire absence of sectarian strife' and how there was 'co-operation of all creeds and parties for the good of the child', coupled with a recognition of 'the fundamental truths of religion and their bearing on one's life and thought'. The reports note the occasional visit of HMI, and the favourable commentary on what they found: in 1938, no less than 10 schools were inspected, and the Reports 'were generally most gratifying to the Education Committee as evidence of the sound work that is being done in the schools and of the conscientious and zealous labour of the pupils'. There are notes of occasional curriculum experiments: for example at Snapethorpe in 1934/35, instruction in cookery and embroidery was given to a class of boys, and woodwork and gardening lessons to girls. Snapethorpe itself was being completed to its fullest extent, and the 1936/37 annual report, signalling the approval of further building work, noted that 'with its special subjects building and demonstration flat, and with 14.7 acres of playground and playing fields, Snapethorpe School will be one of the finest in the country'. But plans for a new school of Arts and Crafts, though approved by the Board of Education, had to be deferred.

Musical, dramatic and sporting activities are faithfully recorded, along with occasional grumbles about the increasing burden of educational administration. In addition to the flood of Acts of Parliament affecting education, Administrative Memoranda and circulars from the Board of Education, the local councillors did their bit to increase the burden on their officers. In the year ending 31 July, 1938, the Education Committee met 20 times, the various standing sub-committees 61 times, minor and special sub-committees 39 times, and other advisory and consultative committees 20 times: 142 meetings to service. It is perhaps surprising that time existed for any developmental work.

Overall, Wakefield appears to have enjoyed a busy and effective education service in the 1930s. The relatively small size of the authority was a positive advantage, in easing both formal and informal contacts between those responsible for its conduct. The development of the Hornsea Seaside School is consistent with the liberal and progressive approach the Council liked to adopt, as it sought to address some of the key public health and educational preoccupations of the period in a pioneering way.

The idea of parties of children from individual schools going on school camps during the summer holidays, or indeed during term time, was not by any means unknown. In his 1934/35 Annual Report, Berry noted that four schools (Trinity Boys, St. Johns' Boys, Westgate Junior and Methodist) had arranged "most successful" holiday camps at Robin Hood's Bay, Humberstone and Colwyn Bay. Nearby schools in the West Riding were doing similar things: in August 1935, for example, the *Wakefield Express* recorded the return of 70 'scholars' of Queen Street Council School in Normanton from a camp in Filey. There was also the practice of sending a group of children away to a seaside camp for a week in term time. This was organised by the Social Service Council with some funding from the Education Committee (though this clearly did not cover all costs: the *Wakefield Express* for 4 July 1936 noted that the Council of Social Service was still seeking assistance with expenses). It benefited 120 children annually (60 boys and 60 girls). The camp was often on the East coast, at Mappleton, about three miles south of Hornsea (this tradition may help explain why the Hornsea area was eventually chosen to be the location of the Seaside School), though the venue was occasionally North Wales. In June, 1936, just as the Education Department was preparing its initial thinking about the establishment of a permanent 'camp school', the *Wakefield Express* for 22 June carried a report of 'Wakefield Children in Camp', this time at Abergele. This was explicitly a holiday, though in charge of teachers, and some of the routines described foreshadowed what would be the practice at Hornsea: the welcoming meal after the coach journey to camp followed by early 'lights out' on the first evening, the daily hut inspections, the gentle attempts to secure some curriculum content to the stay. In this case, the *Express* reported that the first lessons consisted of drawing a route map of the journey to Wales and the commencement of a diary of the visit. Both would be features of the Hornsea curriculum. There was the desire to spend as much time out of doors as possible, unless it was actually raining; in dry spells the children 'scampered down to the beach for physical jerks', and 'games, competitions, sports and swimming' were in prospect if the sun shone. The aim of these camps was, as the *Express* put it, 'to give the children as happy a time as possible'. Those attending had been selected by Teachers and Health Visitors. Others had been assessed as suitable to attend by a Medical Officer. A nurse accompanied the party. Dr Allardice regarded these camps as no substitute for a proper Open Air school, and opined rather grudgingly that the children 'no doubt benefited by their short sojourn by the sea'. Berry was inclined to be more positive and was quite clear that the children were indeed 'wonderfully better for the experience'.

These annual events were in Berry's and the Councillors' minds when on 12 August, 1935 he presented to the Finance and General Purposes Sub-Committee a report on the subject of school camps. That report is unfortunately now lost, but the main ideas can assumed to be reproduced in Berry's Annual Report for 1935/36, which records the proposals the Education Committee eventually agreed.

He envisaged a 'camp school' which would be conducted as a residential elementary school for children from Wakefield's senior schools for 24 weeks in each year, and as a holiday camp for 'debilitated children' during four summer holiday weeks. The school would be occupied by children of one sex at a time, and would be attended by complete school classes or age groups. Eight parties of 80 children, with their teachers, would reside in the camp school for periods of three weeks at a time. _Every child_ (Berry's emphasis) attending a senior school would have 'the opportunity of benefiting by three weeks education in a beautiful and health giving environment and experiencing the valuable corporate life of a residential school' without 'having to qualify by physical debility or parental poverty'. After confirming that the children in camp would 'follow an appropriately

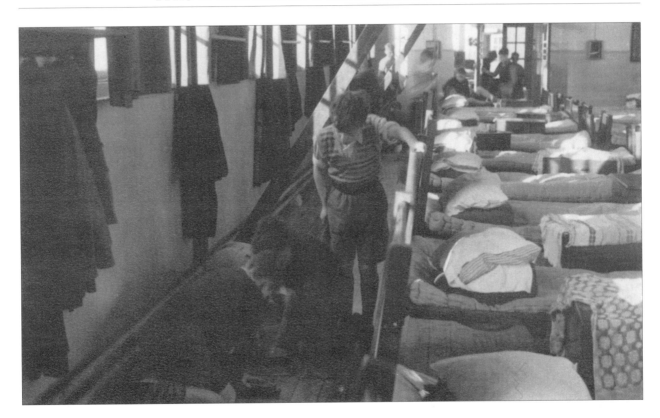

modified curriculum, devised in conjunction with HM Inspector' - after all, it was to be a school, and not, except for a minority of the time it was used, a holiday camp - and that attendances would be recorded as on the registers of the home schools, he returned with renewed emphasis, to the central theme of his vision for the school:

'An essential feature of the proposal is that the camp school should be open to *all* senior school children, and should not be confined to either the poor or the sick. Any such limitations inevitably result in injustice to children themselves. *All* children would benefit by residence at the school. The prevention of debility is better and easier than its cure. The segregation of the sick and poor is neither necessary nor desirable in connection with the scheme. The camp school should be a place to which parents of all classes will gladly send their children when the opportunity is given to them'.

The emphasis is clearly different from what the proponents of the Open Air school regime would have liked: the insistence on inclusiveness and that there should be no distinction between children on the grounds of class or health strikes a progressive note. But the regime which would be followed at Hornsea would, at least in the school's early days, be underpinned by medical considerations: those attending would be examined by a doctor before departure, (though this practice ceased in 1969. Instead, children were seen by the school nurse 'who examined them for personal cleanliness and plantar warts'). For many years the beginning and end of visits to Hornsea would be marked by the ritual of weighing, presumably to help the authorities discern the effect of a healthy lifestyle and a regulated diet had both on the overweight and those who did not 'thrive'. The dietary regime followed plans laid down by the School Medical Officer.

The camp school would benefit the health of those attending (not least from the amount of exercise that the visitors would be required to take, even to reach Hornsea town centre or the beach) but the social benefits would be as great. Allardice himself noted in his Annual Report for 1938/39 'there will be considerable opportunity for the development of social qualities and good natured tolerance in the children concerned. It is, perhaps, true that many of the children in camp really get to know each other properly for the first time in their lives by living together. Such community life at the early age of 12 or 13 will, I feel, do much to broaden the outlook of our future citizens'. Berry's original plan, which was largely followed, took care to ensure that children of poorer families were not discriminated against. Parents were required to pay for their children's subsistence, a sum 'at least equal to what it would cost them to board the child at home for three weeks', but unemployed parents were to be asked only for 'that small sum drawn as unemployment benefit for that child's keep at home'. The 'classlessness' of Hornsea was to have its limits: it remained used largely by senior elementary school children, and later by the Secondary Modern or 'City High' schools: use by pupils from the Grammar schools, whether the Council's own Thornes House or the Foundation Grammar schools, was either occasional, or incidental, if pupils came as part of the music service instrumental courses run from the late 1960s onwards. But it is clear that, contrary to the myths that grew up around the purposes of Hornsea, it was not originally seen primarily as a holiday facility for disadvantaged children: it would benefit every child who attended.

The response of Wakefield's councillors to the idea of a camp school was favourable, and the Director of Education was invited to produce more detailed estimates of building costs and to locate potential sites. It appears that during the latter part of 1935 and in early 1936, the Chairman of the Education Committee, Alderman Burley Johnson, who was to be one of the Seaside School's most loyal supporters, with his deputy and the officers, paid a number of visits to possible school sites. The preferred location, off the Hull Road in Hornsea, a site of 14 acres, overlooking Hornsea Mere and about 1460 yards from the sea shore, was chosen by the spring of 1936.

Hornsea itself had enjoyed a period of steady development as a resort since the opening of the branch railway from Hull in 1864, though of course it was a much older settlement. The Mere had been a notable attraction for a long time, and allowed Hornsea to advertise itself (or to be advertised) as 'Lakeland by the Sea' in railway publications and posters. It boasted of its 'mile long promenade' and its 'glorious golden sands', affording opportunities for 'safe bathing'; and the LNER's *Holiday Handbook* for 1939, records that the town had recently constructed boating lakes at a cost of £8,000. The promenade also offered ornamental gardens, tennis, bowls and putting in the Victoria Gardens; Hall Garth Park, with its famous 'alphabet' gates, provided beautifully wooded walks and a 'sporting' nine hole golf course. Dances and concerts were staged at the Floral Hall, which enjoyed a resident orchestra and a resident concert party. Hornsea summed itself up as 'the ideal family resort', and if it was not overfull of funfairs and arcades (though there were some) it was perhaps a little dismissive of visiting city children to claim that 'there was nothing there'. In fact, Hornsea provided an admirable location for a Seaside School; it offered a range of attractions entirely suitable for the recreation of visiting children; it was very well provided for with Churches and Chapels (five in all, and this mattered in the 1930s, when expectations that the spiritual welfare of children would be looked after at school were more overt than they are, generally, now); the Mere offered tremendous possibilities for nature study; and the town itself contained a range of interesting and historic buildings which could profitably be studied. That it was not over-commercialised was positively an advantage: but it had a life of its own into which the Seaside School would fit comfortably.

By June of 1936, Wakefield's Finance Committee was ready to seek loan sanction from the Ministry of Health (which then oversaw local government affairs) for site purchase. There was some opposition, a number of councillors being reluctant to agree to buy the site until the cost of the buildings had been confirmed, but this was defeated, and in July 1936 the Council approved the loan sanction application. The loan was granted by the Ministry in September 1936, and purchase was completed in January 1937 at a total cost, including legal charges, of £899. The opposition to the purchase of the site seems to have been relatively short lived. In his preface to the Director of Education's Annual Report for the year ended 31 July 1937, Alderman Johnson could write that 'all parties on the council' supported the provision of a 'camp school designed to give health and happiness to hundreds of our scholars'. In fact the positive public attitude to the development of Hornsea can perhaps be discerned from the *Wakefield Express* commentary in its 'Notes and Comments' column for 11 July, 1936: 'We have not the least doubt that the benefit to health which will accrue to children visiting the camp will more than justify the outlay which will be necessary'.

Meanwhile, sketch plans for the buildings had been prepared by the City Housing Architect, Percy Morris, and had been approved by the Board of Education in October, 1936; the final plans and estimates were approved in March 1937, although it appears that the original estimates were felt to be too low, and it was not until the autumn of 1937 that tenders were accepted and building work could commence. The principal contractors were J. H. Taylor and Son, of Hull. The Education Committee established a 'Camp School Sub-Committee' to oversee the building work and the arrangements for furnishing and decorating the new school, and the Director of Education convened a Teachers Advisory Committee to comment on the practical issues involved in running a residential establishment 70 miles away from Wakefield. Their remit covered matters such as the periodicals and library books to be supplied to the school, the rota of schools attending (they suggested that a ballot should decide the order, though for 1938 they agreed that boys should have first call) and how children might be encouraged to save for the weekly boarding charge, pocket money and appropriate clothing. Those of their recommendations which had to be confirmed by the Councillors were not always accepted: they suggested, for example, that quite an extensive range of periodicals, encyclopaedias and library books should be provided (the library to be divided into six sections:- drama, crafts, books suitable for both boys and girls, books suitable for boys only and girls only and books suitable for 'retarded' or less bright children), but this was obviously thought to be extravagant, and the members only agreed to pay for the *Daily Mail* and the *Daily Herald* each day the school was in use, though the *Manchester Guardian* and the *Yorkshire Post* were added for 1939. Library books were eventually to be supplied via the East Riding County Library, though Mr J. H.

Paterson, one of the members of the Advisory Committee, later offered to supply a set of *The Children's Encyclopaedia* at his own expense.

It is difficult to discern how smoothly the building contract ran, although the Camp School Sub-Committee was still taking decisions about such matters as the heating system, the capacity of the kitchen range, and modifications to the construction of the lavatory block, as late as February 1938. The original completion date of 31 March had to be put back by a month and the arrival of the first party of children delayed. Furnishing of the school started from April 1938. The appointment (at a salary of £165 per year) of the Matron of the school, Miss F. Longbottom, who appears to have been employed as a school nurse out of season, was only confirmed by the Education Committee on 29 March, 1938, as was the appointment of Mr and Mrs W. J. B. Beverley as caretaker and cook. The Beverleys were jointly paid £3 per week, plus house, light, coal and food during the season. That meeting of the Education Committee also confirmed the name of the new school: it was not to be called a camp school, but the 'Wakefield Seaside School'. This change may have been occasioned by some public confusion about the nature of the establishment: at the March 1938 Council meeting, the Deputy Chairman of the Education Committee found it necessary to emphasise 'that the school was a building, and there was no question of the children being under canvas'.

The school had cost some £7631 (though there was later to be some dispute with the builders about excess charges, and the final total was nearer £8500: the accounts were not fully settled until very late 1941 or 1942). Furnishings cost about £1150. The layout and development of the grounds was incomplete when the school was first used.

The Seaside School finally opened its doors on 2 May, to a party from the Cathedral Boys' School and the Methodist School. What the Director of Education described as 'this most interesting and valuable development in Health and Education' was at last implemented.

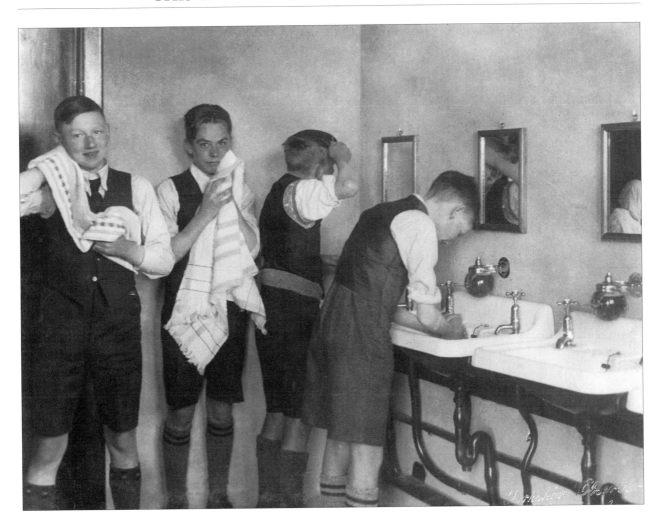

CHAPTER TWO
THERE WE LIVE THREE WEEKS A YEAR

My dad was a Weighman at Parkhill Colliery, that was between Eastmoor and Stanley, he worked there all his life. His mate was a clock weighman, he was employed by the Union to check that my dad was weighing right – in the 1930s the Union didn't trust the coal owners as far as they could chuck them. My dad was on a good wage for a working man, I believe he was paid two pound ten shillings a week when I went to Hornsea in 1938.

I should say that I was in the first lot of lads to go to Hornsea School. I went with my schoolmates from Thornhill Street Methodist School. I can't remember that we did lessons, but we did go on walks around the Mere. We drew birds and trees and the bluebells were out. I also recall that there were vast spaces to run around in. I've been past since and it seems the dormitories we slept in were no more than chicken runs, though everything seems bigger when you are small.

The school wasn't quite finished when we arrived, they were still delivering the beds and there were no chairs, so we stood at the tables for our meals.

The teachers were pleasant, we didn't get chastised, which was a change because at Thornhill Street we had a PT teacher called Miss Moseley who could give you a right slap if you stepped out of line.

Going to Hornsea then was like going to the Mediterranean now. It was clean, there was space and a great sense of togetherness and it was great for a lot of my friends whose dads were out of work, otherwise they wouldn't have had a holiday. I was one of the lucky ones, I had Hornsea and a week at my sister-in-law's at Blackpool.

When you are used to sharing a bed with two sisters and having to have coats on your bed for extra warmth, it was nice to go to Hornsea and sleep in a bed of your own.

Mother often had to go out pea pulling to put food on the table, so the thought of ever going anywhere for a holiday never entered our minds.

I do remember day trips from Westgate Common Workingmen's Club to Cleethorpes, but that was all. I don't think I'd ever been to Leeds before I was an adult. Hornsea School enabled us to get away.

There were two of our teachers with us, Miss Allen and Miss Bates. We had a tuck shop each day, and were allowed to spend 1d some days and 2d another day. This was big money. I remember the suppers mainly because each night was the same - bread and dripping with a cup of cocoa, but we enjoyed it.

On the second Sunday of our holiday our parents came to visit us, so that they could see the school, and if we were homesick we could go home with them. I wouldn't have dared mention that to my mother as it had been hard for her to save the 10 shillings for me to go. We had been taking 6d or one shilling a week to school to pay for the holiday. We had learned a song to sing to them when they came, Miss Allen and Miss Bates wrote it, but we sang it to the tune of 'There is a tavern in the town'.

There is a school near Hornsea Mere, Hornsea Mere
And there we live three weeks a year, weeks a year
We play games and paddle when it's fine, when it's fine
And skip beside the foaming brine, foaming brine.

All at Wakefield come and see us
Though you cannot stay long with us
We love to show you round our Seaside School
Adieu, Adieu.

I was 12 years old, and in December 1938 we lost my dear dad. So I was very kindly given the chance to go half price to Hornsea, it was nine shillings, can you believe that? I sat next to my schoolfriend Pat Riley on the bus, we had a nice ride there and as it was a place I had not been to before, it was all very exciting. The lane towards the school was a picture of flowers, houses, and sheep, it was lovely.

We had arrived for our three weeks holiday, but come night time as I laid down, I thought of Mum on her own, my sister, married and away, and I would never be able to tell my worries again to my dad. So I quietly cried. Two beds away a very nice school friend, Betty Ramsden, came to my side. She went to ask our room teacher if we may have a drink and chat, Miss Holdsworth was like an angel. She put her arm around my shoulders and gave me all I needed.

I went to Hornsea with St John's Girls School in 1938. I can remember the weather being gorgeous and spent a lot of time outdoors playing netball and rounders. We used to go on long walks by the Mere and then down to the beach. We had lessons on the beach sometimes. My mum and my sister came to visit me on the second Sunday, I remember being so pleased to see them as it was the first time I had been away from my family. In fact it was the first time I had had a holiday, our big break used to be on Bank Holiday Monday to Cleethorpes for the day.

We went for three weeks, and it was only the second time I had seen the sea, the first time was at Cleethorpes on a day trip with Balne Lane WMC. We did lessons, but mainly Nature Studies. We were fortunate, because our three weeks covered the Whitsuntide holidays, so there wasn't much schooling. While we were there, some of the boys were acting about in the dormitory and one lad, Melvine Wiltshire, finished up with his arm through the glass in the door. He had a lot of stitches in it, and had an extended stay there.

CHAPTER THREE
A SPLENDID ADVERTISEMENT

The Education Committee may have been a little late in setting some of the staffing and furnishing details of its new school, but it had with some skill primed the public as to its aims and functions by circulating in early March 1938 what amounted to a prospectus, complete with a rather fanciful artist's impression of what the school would look like when it was finished. It noted that 'already some parents are preparing for the opportunity (of going to Hornsea) which they hope will be extended to their children', and that 'in certain schools, children have been saving through their school savings association or school bank so that the contributions towards their three weeks maintenance may be ready for payment to the Education Authority when the time comes. It is confidently anticipated that parents generally will give their children every help and encouragement in the matter, so that no child will be disappointed'. The contributions referred to had been set at £1 (five shillings per week for food, and five shillings for fares). Parents were asked to pay this amount; though they were able to offer less, very few did so. The first party to visit Hornsea included a few children from the Bede House in College Grove, a home for Orphan and Poor Boys, who attended the Cathedral School in Brook Street. Their contributions were paid by Mr Pinchbeck, the owner of the tobacconists and hairdresser in Brook Street, and Fr Clarke, of St. John's parish.

After reproducing the principles behind the school discussed in Chapter One above, the prospectus described the buildings in some detail. The prospectus then went on to describe how the school would run, in terms which set the tone for Hornsea for much of its early history. The school would be 'in charge of' a teacher and a Matron. The former would have 'all the authority and responsibilities' of a Headteacher, and would be assisted by the three teachers expected to travel with each visiting party. Those teachers would also be responsible for the recreational activities of the children and for the discipline and corporate life of the school. Saturdays and Sundays would be devoted to 'excursions, games and recreation'. Religious education 'will occupy the usual place in the school timetable', with each day opening and closing with family prayer. 'On Sundays, each child would attend service at the place of worship selected by his parents, thus ensuring the 'continuity of each child's personal religious life'. 'Services in school in substitution thereof' were not to be allowed. (In time, that rule was to be quietly disregarded, especially on wet Sunday mornings). Parents were assured of the availability of a 'nutritious and carefully balanced diet', and of the availability of both a sick room (which it was 'hoped would be but rarely used') and 'efficient medical attention' (in the event provided by local general practitioners and the Hornsea War Memorial Cottage Hospital). As much work as possible was to be done in the open air, though two classrooms were provided; and a recreation room was to be used for 'games, wireless listening and other indoor activities'.

The information thus provided provoked a lot of press attention, as it was no doubt intended to, and much coverage was enthusiastic. The *Yorkshire Observer* of 4 March 1938, as well as noting that the Hornsea School was one of the first of its type in the country and that its opening was 'eagerly awaited' by parents, will have gratified the Council by recording that 'Wakefield's progressive educational policy is one of which the city is greatly proud' and that the experiment of building a summer school at Hornsea 'has aroused much favourable comment'. The *Hull Daily Mail* of 11 March 1938, under the headline 'West Riding money for Hornsea', noted that 'Wakefield is one of the first authorities to provide proper school accommodation by the sea where the ordinary curriculum can be continued by the children, but instead of having all the disadvantages of a town's environment during the summer they will...derive great benefit from the health giving sea air'. It concluded that 'Hornsea should be proud to be chosen for one of the first schools of this kind...the advantages of the school to Hornsea are obvious: but apart from the fact that many local workmen have received additional work in its erection, the school...will be a great advertisement for the healthiness of the resort, especially in the West Riding'.

Press interest in the seaside school continued up to the formal opening on 12 May, 1938.

The first party of visitors was photographed for the *Yorkshire Observer*, both preparing to leave for Hornsea, with every sign of enthusiasm, and then settling into the dormitories: some were even shown washing themselves!

The *Wakefield Express* of 7 May, 1938, in covering the previous Thursday's Council

meeting, reported Alderman Johnson's bulletin on the first day's use of Hornsea: 'that the scholars had started off in working order, that they had got on splendidly, that the food was good and that the children were thoroughly happy'. Not surprisingly, Alderman Johnson suggested that this information 'might well induce a spirit of optimism as to the success of the school'. The *Express* was gracious enough to comment that notwithstanding some earlier misgivings as to the wisdom of going ahead with the Hornsea venture, 'we have not the slightest doubt that before the Summer is over, the ratepayers generally will come to the conclusion that the outlay involved was money well spent'.

The spirit of optimism referred to by Alderman Johnson was much in evidence when the official opening took place on Thursday, 12 May, 1938, faithfully recorded by the local and regional press, from which the following account is condensed. The ceremony was performed by the Mayor of Wakefield, Alderman Tom Crowe. That he was able to be present at all was a minor miracle. He had been struck in the eye by a tennis ball the previous weekend, and subsequently had required stitches in his leg when a sheet of plate glass fell on him at work (he was employed as a coachbuilder by the LMS Railway). There were no mishaps, however, when he opened the main doors of the school with a silver key, or when he made his speech, saying that 'it was a splendid thing that children coming from a smoke ridden atmosphere like that of Wakefield would have the privilege of spending three weeks in such attractive and clean surroundings, and would gain not only health and strength but a degree of learning also'. In order to have alert minds it was necessary to have healthy bodies. There was a good deal of talk about a C3 nation, but 'if there is anything which will lay the foundations for an A1 nation, it is to be found in schools of this kind'. The other speakers echoed his sentiments. Alderman Johnson paid tribute to the Board of Education for allowing Wakefield to experiment with the Seaside School - reflecting the negotiations which would have been required both to obtain the capital funding to allow the school to be built, and the discussion over the curriculum to be followed. The HMI who had approved the schemes of work, Colonel FDW Bendall, CMG, was present at the opening, in what one might suspect was fitting recognition of his assistance in getting the school established. Of course, the Hornsea Urban District Council was represented in strength, and its Chairman, M. F.G. Mather, welcomed the guests. His speech nicely mixed wider policy sentiments with an eye to local advantage. 'Education was necessary', he said, 'but health had to be looked after before its benefit could be felt'. That reason in itself commended the Seaside School. He added that the site chosen for the Seaside School 'is one of the best in Hornsea, but we have plenty more like it. If any other authority would like to establish a school here we shall be delighted to help them'. He went on to remind his audience that not only was Hornsea's beach 'second to none', but also that the health service was on as high a plane as in any other town of a similar size, and that, (to clinch the argument!), the local rates were 'very moderate'.

The boys attending the school had been kept otherwise occupied while the opening ceremony was conducted, but the *Yorkshire Observer* noted a 'happy diversion' when the 'stress laid by the speakers on the health value of studies by the sea was emphasised by the buoyant tread of 80 odd boys in residence...as they returned from an excursion to the beach. The boys...were full of high spirits and eagerly told the visitors of their happy experiences in the sunshine at the school. For some of them it was their first glimpse of the sea and one glance at their bright faces was sufficient to convince the most sceptical of the success of the Wakefield experiment'.

What is interesting is that the opening of Hornsea was seen as having some national significance, though Wakefield never claimed the school as unique. The *School Government Chronicle and Education Review* for June 1938 carried a lengthy article, with plans and photographs, making the point that the new school was one of very few to be planned and built as a residential Summer school; and *Education* magazine also featured the school prominently in its edition of July 29, 1938. The national interest in Hornsea continued after the War. As will be described later, the school reopened briefly in 1947, but resumed for a full season in 1948. The reopening was marked by the *Daily Mirror*, on 16 April, which published an attractive photograph of a group of girls and their teachers studying encrustations on a groyne on Hornsea beach; *Picture Post*, a mass circulation weekly, ran a long article on 7 August, 1948, and the *Yorkshire Observer* covered one of the August visits by boys from the Cathedral and the Methodist schools. As late as 1955, the *News Chronicle* felt it worth running a story on the school, featuring a visit by girls from Snapethorpe Secondary Modern School. In 1948 also, the school featured in a film in the 'This Modern Age' series produced by the Rank Organisation called 'Education for Living', helping to illustrate what the film-makers took to be the purpose of the changes in Education introduced by the 1944 Education Act, 'to secure for children a happier childhood and a better start in life'. The camera crew arrived on 1 September, 1948 to film a party from the Cathedral and the Methodist schools. The weather prevented much filming initially: an indoor lesson on letter writing would not have made good cinema, but on the following day, it was possible to record activities by the Mere and on the beach. The film was premiered in April 1949, alongside 'Passport to Pimlico'. This was not, of course, the first time the school had been filmed. The Council had decided to commemorate the opening of the school with a film of its own, 'An Adventure in Education'. It was an account of the building, opening and activities of the Seaside School. The Director of Education is seen studying plans for the school, and discussing them with Dr Allardice, there are shots of the opening ceremony and glimpses of the children at work and play, in the dormitories, on the school fields and having fun in the showers. The film, which only survives now in a heavily edited and poor quality video transcript, was reviewed in the Monthly Bulletin of the British Film Industry for May 1939. The reviewer noted that it appeared 'primarily intended for local propaganda', and commented on the tedium of the scenes of the opening ceremony 'except to parents and friends of the persons concerned', but it was recommended for showing the 'value of fresh sea air to young children from an industrial town'. Wakefield would also have been pleased with the comment that the film 'is an object lesson in what can be done by an Education Authority with vision'. It is hard to be sure how far this vision was shared in the wider world of Education. That Wakefield was a leading part of a broader movement is clear: just over a year after Hornsea opened, the Government passed the 'Camps Act' (2 & 3 Geo 6 Ch. 22), which provided for the construction of camps 'of a permanent character' with Government finance channelled through the National Camps Corporation (NCC), whose Managing Director, Sir Edward Howarth, was Deputy Secretary at the Board of Education between 1937 and 1939: that is, during the period when the plans for Hornsea were coming to fruition. The aim of the NCC was to provide camps in country or coastal areas for use by school parties in relays or by holidaymakers in peacetime. In the event of War, it was thought they might house people driven from the cities by bombing, and some were in fact selected for use by secondary schools relocated from urban areas. There are some indications that a similar use might have been contemplated for Hornsea. Wakefield's Elementary School Sub-Committee on 20 November, 1939 had a report on a visit to Hornsea by a Mr R. Stuart of the Ministry of Health who 'expressed his satisfaction with the premises and congratulated Wakefield on providing so fine a camp school'. He promised to let the authority know whether the premises were likely to be required by the Ministry: in fact it did not take long for them to decide that the school would not be needed, unsurprisingly given its location on the east coast, which was thought vulnerable to invasion. But Hornsea would have shared the disadvantages also discerned in respect of the NCC's premises: it was not designed for permanent or year-round occupation, (the original heating system at Hornsea was sometimes not equal to the demands of cold Springs or Autumns), it would have lacked facilities for indoor recreation in Winter, and had limited teaching space and insufficient private accommodation for teachers - especially over long periods. Those NCC camps that were completed on the outbreak of war were similar to Hornsea in style, but much larger. Each camp was on a site of 20 - 40 acres, with a hall, a block of six classrooms, a dining hall (to seat 400), with kitchen and stores, six dormitories for 58 children each (using two-tier iron bedsteads) and a teacher's room at each end, separate lavatory blocks, and accommodation for the camp manager and the teacher in charge of the visiting pupils. The buildings were of cedar wood. Hornsea is like a scaled down version of an NCC camp. What was unusual about Hornsea was that it arose directly from local authority initiative.

Whether the camp school 'movement' would have developed had it not been for the

Second World War must be a matter for speculation. It appears that the NCC camps that survived the War were leased to LEAs and at least for a time were well appreciated. Middlesex LEA for example leased two camp schools from the NCC in Hampshire, where both boys and girls aged 11 - 15 from the secondary modern schools 'spent a term, and in many cases two or more terms under the healthiest possible conditions and with full opportunities to explore the natural and historical environment of the schools while continuing their normal education'. Middlesex also made arrangements for parties of children to visit a holiday camp at New Romney for a fortnight each Summer term. The children were said to 'benefit by the great historical associations of the neighbourhood'. Middlesex, a very large LEA, sent some 3000 children to camp each year. Wakefield County Borough sent between 700 and 1200 children to Hornsea, depending on the length of season, which proportionally to the number of children in the Authority was a much greater use of the 'camp' approach, but Wakefield appears never to have considered stays of longer than 3 weeks. Nearer to home, the West Riding County Council used an NCC camp at Bewerley Park, near Pateley Bridge. Here, the NCC retained responsibility for the domestic side of the camp, while the LEA provided the educational input. Initially, the West Riding sent groups to Bewerley Park for a month at a time. The 'open air life and regular habits' of the camp were said to 'do much to improve personal habits as well as health'. The West Riding recorded that 'washing, bathing, feeding and sleeping under other than parental discipline is salutary for many children; bed making and even shoe cleaning are new to some as part of a daily routine'. Exactly the same might have been written of Hornsea. (In fact it was: an article that appeared in the *Yorkshire Post* in August 1948 noted on a visit to Hornsea that 'on the first day we discovered 58 ways of making a bed.') The West Riding also used to have the children attending Bewerley Park weighed on arrival and departure and recorded the average weight gain - as was done at Hornsea. The County Council bought Bewerley Park in 1956, and, feeling that the need for what it now regarded as a 'welfare centre' was no longer paramount, converted it into a boarding school with an emphasis on field studies work and other outdoor pursuits, with great success. The West Riding changed the character of Bewerley Park rather more rapidly than Wakefield even considered, at least until local government reorganisation in 1974.

These examples confirm that Hornsea was not unique in its concepts and its aims. But it was - and is - a rarity, and it is probable that the Second World War ensured that it would stay a rarity, as a Seaside School owned and managed by an LEA. For all that the *Yorkshire Post* in August 1948 could write (probably echoing a briefing given by Wakefield) that 'so many other local authorities are casting envious glances at Hornsea and impatiently waiting for the day when building restrictions are relaxed', the need for permanent school accommodation to replace War-damaged schools and to meet the needs of a rising population effectively prevented Hornsea's replication. And by the time that building restrictions *were* removed, the need for a facility like Hornsea, at least as a purpose built school, would have seemed less obvious.

But in 1938, with the school just open, it stood as the realisation of the 'dreams and hopes of Wakefield's educationalists' and a 'splendid advertisement', not just for Hornsea, as the local papers proclaimed, but for Wakefield as a progressive local authority.

CHAPTER FOUR
PIT BOOTS SHONE LIKE DIAMONDS

When we arrived at Hornsea, we all walked in uniform across the playing field, over the old railway and on the road into town. Very smart we all looked in our black blazers, grey trousers and green, black and white ties. It was a hot day so we were allowed to take off our blazers while we familiarised ourselves with the town.

Our days came and went. I hated the morning cleaning of each dorm. The inspections as we stood beside our beds were very army-like. My new pit-boots shone like diamonds and I picked up a few points for our dorm. It was great to share our days together, playing cricket, five-a-side football, but on Sunday we had to endure a two hour Church service.

We got plenty of free time, in the afternoons. I would go into the town with a few friends and we'd spend the money we were allowed per day and enjoy the go-karts and slot machines. In the evening we'd don our PE gear and run around the bank of the Mere. On the Monday we all walked to the Pottery and were shown the way clay was made into squirrels, rabbits and mugs. These items were to decorate most people's sideboards and shelves back home.

The then 'showers' were always cool, and we all ran across from our dorms with towels wrapped round our skinny bodies to endure a wash. One night the fire siren was sounded, and we all in a panic ran into the field in our pyjamas to be accounted for. Just a practice.

On the 13th, we were all told ghost stories and frightened ourselves to death as Mr Beardsell said 'only that month the caretaker had reported a sighting of the Blue Lady who walks over the murky waters of the Mere on this night'. I remember that we all said 'rubbish', but that night two lads weed their beds. Lovely days. Memories of carefree, innocent lads working and playing as a team.

Although it was a holiday it was an educational one, with lessons in the morning. Not long ones, always interesting and enjoyed because you knew that after lunch you had afternoons doing interesting things. We had visits to Beverley Minster, walks around the Mere, and walks around the school, collecting wild flowers and making notes of everything of interest so you could write a really good essay next day.

Saturday and Sundays were days of leisure, Saturday a walk into Hornsea to spend your pocket money. I remember buying sweet cigarettes with my friend and pretending to smoke them, then being seen and accused of smoking. Lucky for us we had not eaten them all. We had visits to Hornsea Pottery, watched them making all the different items, then going to the reject shop and buying gifts. I bought a small boxer dog and a poodle.

We went swimming and I swam over a breakwater and cut my leg, boy did it bleed, so I had to use the towel I had with me. When we arrived back at the school I put the towel into soak in the sink in the toilet block, left it and also left the tap on. You can guess. I flooded the block so my friend and I had to mop up, as I was the dormitory monitor this did not go down very well at all. It was soon forgiven and forgotten when we started to rehearse for our concert for the last night. We did song and dance routines and acted as film stars. I managed to have a white bikini and as I was blonde I was Marilyn Monroe, saying the famous words 'Gentlemen prefer blondes'.

The ablutions were in another hut, with sinks, toilets and showers all in a row. We all queued up to use them in turn. The dining room was larger, and I remember having cocoa and mucky fat (or dripping as it is called today) for supper. We had lessons in the morning, then after dinner we walked and walked. Some days over the railway to the sea, collecting pebbles and seaweed shells for lessons the next morning. Some days we walked round the fields on a nature walk collecting wild flowers to press the next day. We were always tired when we got back at teatime. After the teacher put the lights out, and all was clear, we all got out our goodies for a midnight feast. On another day a walk down a steep hill to the Mere. We had a trip on a boat, round the island looking for the Hornsea monster, again writing the next morning and making up stories of the monster.

I went to Hornsea Seaside School when I was almost 12 years old for two weeks during the school holidays. We went on the Monday and came back on the Monday two weeks later. At first I was not too keen on going and leaving home for two whole weeks. It cost my parents 6/- for the time I was there. There was a full bus to go and it was an enjoyable journey. When we got there we were allocated to different dormitories. Mine was Hornsea and we soon made friends with the other girls. We went to the dining room for our meals and met the matron who was a real tartar. The teachers were good. Mrs Priestley was our dormitory teacher and Mr Turton was the overall head. He used to go in the recreation room at night and before he went to bed he used to tell us stories about 'a man in the bowler hat'. Each night this used to end with him almost getting into some sort of exciting happening. The next night he got out of the scrape he was in. We never did get to know in the end what happened to him.

I remember having to pick weeds when one night we had the dormitory in a bit of an uproar with one of the girls telling us funny stories. The tartar turned up and made everyone stand by their beds, even the ones who had been asleep. Picking the weeds was a punishment.

All in all it was an experience I have not forgotten. When we got there we got weighed. I was once again in trouble as I weighed less and matron wanted to know the reason why. How the heck did I know? We got home about lunchtime and both my mum and dad were there to meet me. It was great to be home. I then had to start my new school, St John's Girls, the next day and straight away had an exam to see which form I was to go in. What a home coming!

I enjoyed being at Hornsea especially when we were in the dormitory together and one of the other girls was sleepwalking or pretending to be sleepwalking. We didn't have a lot of pocket money but would enjoy going to any shop to buy sweets. We went into the Floral Hall and it was there that we sang and danced the Lambeth Walk. Some of the girls I was with at Hornsea and at Ings Road Central School I still see occasionally in Wakefield and we still stop and chat about old times. One of the odd memories I have is that we had to take shirts to iron and to this day I still like ironing shirts which most people, especially my daughters, don't particularly like even though they have them to do.

CHAPTER FIVE
THE CHILDREN WERE THOROUGHLY HAPPY

In its first full season, the Seaside School was attended by 279 boys and 221 girls. Boys were in residence from 2nd May to 31st July; the school was used until 22nd August as a 'holiday home for those younger children specially selected by the School Medical Officer as being physically delicate or debilitated'. This holiday superseded the camps previously provided via the Social Service Council. Girls were then in residence until the end of the season on 22nd October. The Teacher in Charge while the boys attended was Mr A. Sykes, BA, Cathedral Boys' School, and while the girls were there, Miss K. Hawkins, Art Mistress at Snapethorpe Council Senior School. They were resident throughout their half of the season: in future, it would prove increasingly difficult to recruit someone willing to be exiled to the east coast for three months or so, and it became usual for one of the staff with each of the visiting parties to be in charge for the duration of each visit. At various times in the early 1950s, Messrs Armstrong, Edwards and Watson, and Miss Perkins, were in charge for the Boys' and Girls' seasons: but such appointments became the exception.

The timetable was the same for boys and girls and provided for a busy and regimented day, emphasising that during term-time Hornsea was a school, not a holiday camp. On Mondays - Saturdays, the day began at 7am; prayers were held at 7.45, breakfast was at 8 am and following breakfast the children tidied the dormitories. There was a brief period of free time before lessons began at 9.15; they continued until noon, with a brief break. Dinner followed at 12.30, and the children rested for half an hour from 1.15pm. Lessons began again at 2pm and continued until tea at 4.30. Free time lasted from 5pm until 6pm and then there was a brief 'non-educational period' before supper, toothbrush drill, prayers at 8.45 and lights out at 9.15pm. (Much to the disappointment of some children: they felt it unnatural to go to bed in what was still daylight.) Lessons were not held on Saturdays and Sundays; on Sundays, the children were allowed to lie in until 8am but much of Sunday morning was taken up with church attendance. The Teacher in Charge had discretion over planning weekend activities, but the second Sunday in residence saw visits from parents, who before returning to Wakefield, were able to tour the school and see 'the conditions under which the children lived'. Mr Sykes records that they 'expressed themselves as delighted' by what they saw and that he received several letters of appreciation from the visiting parents.

The pattern set in 1938 substantially survived the war and continued for much of the Seaside School's life until local government reorganisation in 1974. In practice, some latitude over timing of lessons was always allowed, or taken, and the vagaries of east coast weather meant that teachers usually tried to take advantage of fine, warm days to go to the beach or do other outdoor activities irrespective of the demands of the timetable. Visits and excursions were also not confined to weekends. The boys were, at least initially, not allowed to go out on their own: the Mere in particular was out of bounds.

In his report on the season, Mr Sykes noted that 'school life was extremely well organised from the beginning'. The dormitories were named 'Beverley, Hornsea and Hull', and each dormitory had a member of staff in charge and an elected captain. The occupants of each dormitory had to have bed, kit and building ready for inspection by 9am daily when the Teacher in Charge came round and gave marks for tidiness: the ceremony of inspection remains a feature of Hornsea life up to the present day. The pupils not only had to clean and tidy the dormitories: not infrequently in Hornsea history they have been invited to help with other tasks around the site, especially when staff shortages occurred. At various times, pupils have helped mark out pitches on the field, remove stones from the field in preparation for mowing, help bring in a hay crop from the field and dig the gardens: and on one occasion in August 1954, a group of boys from Ings Road had to help the Teacher in Charge to wire 20 spring mattresses to prepare for a larger than expected intake.

The curriculum was weighted towards outdoor lessons, both for girls and boys, and had a 'practical nature'. For both boys and girls, Religious Observance and Instruction was heavily emphasised. Domestic duties were not allowed to interfere with prayers or religious instruction. Even in the Summer holidays morning and evening prayers were performed with the 'sincerest reverence'.

Sunday attendance at church was insisted on, and in the case of the boys, they were encouraged to go to Holy Communion. In the school itself 'the useful religious art of hymn singing was not neglected'.

The school had been equipped with sports material, which was evidently well used, and inter-school matches were arranged with Hornsea Council School for both boys and girls.

The Seaside School appears to have introduced Rugby League to Hornsea: a game was played 'in front of many spectators'. Visits were paid by the boys to Catfoss Aerodrome and Hull Docks: both boys and girls visited the Parish Church and the game reserves at Wassand. The girls also attended a 'cub hunting' meet in the Autumn and made more use of the Hornsea Mere and its surrounds for nature rambles, collecting interesting examples of flowers, fruits and leaves 'and there was much friendly rivalry between the dormitories to procure the best collection'.

Leisure time was fully occupied. Dormitory concerts and singsongs were frequently arranged, and the school had been provided with table tennis, draughts, chess, dominoes, bagatelle, darts and billiards. The East Riding Library Service provided books. The girls held informal dances, and visited the cinema and the Floral Hall on the sea front. Sea bathing was enjoyed when the weather was clement; otherwise the school had use of the Granville Court Hotel swimming pool. One member of the first party remembers that they had to pay 2d for use of the pool but that 'it was so cold we came out and got our 2d back'. The girls' period of residence in 1938 coincided with the Munich crisis: 'to alleviate any tension that was felt, a fancy dress party was held, and the girls were so interested in preparing costumes and entertainments that all fears vanished'.

Miss Hawkins commented that 'the chief gain derived by the children from residence in the school appears to me to be in their opportunities for social learning'. Mr Sykes put it less bluntly but he clearly had similar views. Both Teachers in Charge commented on the importance of making meal times pleasant social occasions:

'The cultivation of good table manners was not overlooked. With each party of boys an effort was made to include ideas of courtesy and to encourage normal conversation. In each case this effort was successful'.

'After initial experiments a system was adopted which involved the use of day to day table servers with regard to the actual serving of meals by the boys. This system was proved to combine dignity with efficiency...'

Those were the words of Mr Sykes. Similar efforts were made by Miss Hawkins:

'Girls of all types, from different classes and from varied home environments, had to live a communal life entirely different from anything which they had experienced before.

They came into closer contact with their teachers...and discovered that they could be at their ease with them. This attitude was largely the result of the arrangements in the dining hall. Each table was served by the two girls at the foot of the table who, for the following meal, sat at the opposite end...on either side of the teacher and, by her, were encouraged to talk in a natural manner. It was noticed...that in serving the meals the girls developed in dignity and poise. Everyone took great pride in being well mannered at the table, in the spotlessness of the table cloths and in providing attractive table decorations of wild flowers and leaves or berries'.

Nothing was neglected: 'habits of orderliness and cleanliness extended to the bath and washbowls which the girls were trained to leave in a clean condition'. Sykes was satisfied to record that 'in school, at meals, in the streets, and at church, conduct was above reproach. The exceptional tone of the school was commented upon by more than one visitor'.

The boys particularly, and the staff accompanying them, seem to have been conscious that they were pioneers, and the initial party does appear to have had some difficulties to overcome. The first meal (consisting of bread and butter and salad) had to be eaten standing up, as the dining hall chairs had not arrived, and other catering problems may not have been resolved by the time the school opened: Sykes indirectly refers to these, and remarks that 'when (they) were overcome, the food became highly satisfactory in quantity and quality'. (The recollection of one of the boys in the first party is that the cook left after two or three days, after a dispute with either the LEA or the teacher in charge.) The buildings themselves presented one or two problems: they weren't ideally suited to the robust handling they received from some 70 lively adolescents, and a number of accidents in the first season proved the unwisdom of installing glass panelled doors. One of those accidents appears to have resulted in legal proceedings being taken.

That 'the constant well arranged activities kept the boys busy and happy' (and the girls also) was no doubt true, but the Hornsea experience, in 1938 as in 1998, was demanding on the staff. As Sykes noted 'the duties were not small, lasting as they did some 15 hours per day'; and 'periods of bad weather added greatly to the work of the staff whose constant duty it was to keep the boys happily busy inside'. Their efforts were appreciated. Mr A. Lancaster, from Snapethorpe School, who was in the second party to visit, recalls that 'the staff went out of their way to see we enjoyed ourselves and got on with us well'. Similar demands were of course made on those staff who supervised the holiday periods. Mr J. H. Paterson, who was in charge of the first holiday party, recorded his 'deep indebtedness to those who assisted, giving loyalty and co-operation and evincing that good temper on all occasions, even far into the night, which wins the best response from youngsters'. He singled out Mr Leonard Shaw, Mr Percy Shaw who 'knows how to handle lads', and Mr. Corston, whose 'patience with the boys was a trait to be envied'. Mr Percy Shaw was the Physical Instructor, and a regular member of the team of staff running the Seaside School in the years after the war: he was remembered as 'a giant of a man'.

The officers of the Council were clear that the Seaside School was worthwhile. Dr Allardice wrote an article, which has been preserved in the scrapbook the Education Department kept about the early days of Hornsea, in which he waxed lyrical about the school and what it was doing. For him, Hornsea represented 'a new conception of the comprehensive meaning of education'. The impression he gained from visiting the boys was 'they form a large, happy family...they were all brimming over with good humour and seemed to have found a new zest in life'. To some 'the better conditions of living' act almost without exception as a tonic...both mentally and physically'. He went further: 'There is probably nothing which brings out the best in youth like camp life, where a healthy competition even if unobtrusive is in existence all the time and where the boy or girl who may be below average intellectually has an opportunity of commanding considerable respect from his more brilliant fellows by the quality of his behaviour and by putting into practice many little...applications of the common sense he or she frequently possesses in greater than

ordinary measure. It may be true that the intellectual idol is in danger of falling from his pedestal unless he looks to his laurels practically, but even that may not be bad for him or her concerned as it tends to promote striving towards all round development rather than a lop sided braininess'.

Allardice's enthusiasm for Hornsea did not prevent him, in his annual report for 1938/39, from reverting to one of his long standing themes, that the Council should still invest in an Open Air school for the permanent benefit of delicate children; and he reminded his readers of the benefit of designing all schools on open air principles. For him, Hornsea was, for all its qualities, still only second best. However, he also recorded a study of the weight of children taken before going to camp and on the day of their return. The children on average gained about 2lbs while at Hornsea, and a further 2½lbs after another three months. Weight gain was supposed to indicate the beneficial effects of a good diet and frequent exercise; but the statistics showed such wide variations that the average was almost meaningless. The true benefit of Hornsea was found elsewhere:

'Interviewing these children brings out that (they) enjoyed themselves enormously. This period of mental weal is surely more significant than the gain or loss of a few pounds, which at best is a mere pointer towards the physical benefit of the period at camp'.

A sample of the menu devised for the first season is reproduced opposite. It clearly provides fuel for the active regime children were expected to follow at Hornsea!

An interesting sidelight on the Seaside School in its first season is found in the magazine of the long-demolished Holy Trinity Church, whose day school boys were in residence in June 1938; two parishioners visited the boys and recorded their impressions. They noted that the three-week stay only cost £1, but felt that 'far higher is the value of the constant life of the boarding school, with mental discipline, wider polish of boy upon boy and regular meals, hours and bed times'. They liked the 'springy beds with light mattresses' used in the school, and commended the buildings, with the exception of the glass folding doors (which had recently caused one of the parishioners, one Tom Caton, such a serious wrist injury that he had to go to hospital for an operation by a specialist from Hull) and 'the really

MEAL	MONDAY	TUESDAY	WEDNESDAY	THURSDAY	FRIDAY	SATURDAY	SUNDAY
BREAKFAST	Porridge with Sugar or Syrup *$^1/_2$ pint Cocoa Bread and Butter +One Apple	Cereal with fresh Milk++ $^1/_2$ pint of Tea Bread and Butter Kipper	Porridge with Sugar or Syrup $^1/_2$ pint of Milk Bread and Butter One Apple	Cereal with fresh Milk $^1/_2$ pint of Tea Bread and Butter Fresh Herring	$^1/_2$ pint of Milk Bread and Butter ** Fish Cakes Marmalade	Cereal with fresh Milk, $^1/_2$pint Cocoa Bread Fresh Bacon Marmalade	Porridge $^1/_2$ pint of Tea Bread and Butter Banana Marmalade
DINNER	Meat and Vegetable Hot Pot Steamed Pudding and Custard	Shepherd's Pie Boiled Turnip Bread and Butter Pudding	Fried Liver Peas Baked Potatoes Rice Pudding	Brown Stew Beans Cabbage Potatoes Steamed Pudding and Custard	Vegetable Soup Fish Pie Apple	Meat Pie Boiled Carrots Baked Potatoes Jam Roll	Roast Beef Yorkshire Pudding Potatoes Greens Rice Pudding
TEA	$^1/_2$ pint of Tea Bread, Butter, Jam Vegetable Salad	$^1/_2$ pint of Milk Bread, Butter, Banana Jam	$^1/_2$ pint of Tea Bread and Butter ** Potted Meat	$^1/_2$ pint of Milk Bread and Butter Orange and Banana Salad	$^1/_2$ pint of Tea Bread and Butter Jam or Syrup Stewed Prunes and Custard	$^1/_2$ pint of Tea Bread and Butter Jam Apple	$^1/_2$ pint of Tea Bread and Butter Jam Sweetcake
SUPPER	Horlicks Malted Milk $^1/_2$ pint Water Biscuits and Butter	Cocoa $^1/_2$ pint Bread and Butter $^1/_2$ oz Cheese	Horlicks Malted Milk Water Biscuits and Butter	Horlicks Malted Milk Water Biscuits and Butter	Cocoa Bread and Butter $^1/_2$ oz Cheese	Horlicks Malted Milk Water Biscuits and Butter	Prepared Lemonade Plain Sweetened Biscuits (e.g. Rich Tea, Marie, Abernethy, Pat-a-Cake)

+	Apples to be washed. Skins edible.	++	Cereals include Shredded Wheat, Post Toasties, Force, etc.
*	Cocoa to be made with equal parts of fresh milk and water.	**	To be prepared on the premises.

extraordinary noticeboard outside' (which can be seen on some of the photographs reproduced in this book, and which seems to have been regarded as over-assertive). They recorded the 'delightful' tone of the school and the 'Latin grace, joined in by all'; 'the food was a joy, and the manners at table so good'.

The staff were described as 'self sacrificing', uncomplaining about their 14 hour days.

The visitors approved of early rising 'with the strap awaiting the laggard'; 'Awake my soul, slap, slap, slap' and of the bedside prayers, 'an education to many'. They suggested that a 1d per week subscription from the boys in residence would provide the common room with papers and comics, and thought that 'a bell hung on an open air belfry on a rafter would give a note to the school'. But they clearly liked the place, and conveyed the impression that the children were enjoying it as well.

There is, in fact, something of a feeling of innocent joy about the published material on Hornsea's first season, which sometimes is recovered in the accounts of later seasons as recorded in logbooks. Wakefield had created something that it thought was going to work, that would have 'far reaching effects for good'. Allardice wrote, in commenting that the school's position meant that the activities carried out would cause no disturbance to local residents:

'It seems a pity, all the same, that the hearty, spontaneous laughter, so infectious within a given range, is prevented from spreading and causing happiness to others by the very conditions it is so desirable to have in a camp like this'.

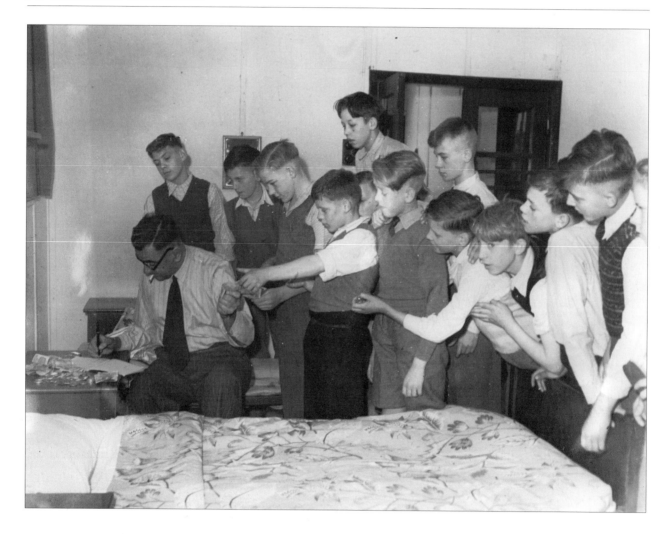

CHAPTER SIX
RACE ACROSS TO THE ABLUTIONS BLOCK

Bear in mind that neither Rebecca nor I are, or more importantly were, remotely musical. Yet here we were with violin and box cello being sent away to a music school for who knows how long!

The next flashback is of myself, wearing deep purple polyester nightie, lying in the first of a long row of beds in a dormitory. It's daylight and a rather concerned adult is sat on a chair next to my bed pleading with me to eat. Who knows how long I had been in this state but the anxiety in this poor woman's voice lives with me to this day. I told her that the only food I would consider eating was a dry Ryvita, which I was duly given.

The weekend arrived without anything but Ryvita having passed my lips. Rebecca and I were packed and ready for our return to Wakefield. Mum and Dad arrived as promised but I sensed that all was not well. We were not to return home.

It was always the case Mum made us do things we didn't particularly want to do (like music lessons!) and Dad was always the fun guy. But on this (and I am struggling to think of any other) occasion the politics of the family had been reversed. Dad was playing the 'hard man' and we were not going to be allowed home.

The strange thing is that I wasn't having a particularly miserable time; in fact, looking back, I think I was quite enjoying myself. The highlights of the 'holiday' were the daily trips to the souvenir shop at Hornsea Pottery. Rebecca and I spent the whole time trying to decide which astrological star sign ring we were going to buy. It had obviously never occurred to us that we each had our own sign – I'd taken a fancy to one with fish on it, even though my birthday is in August.

The most exciting incident was the brief exposure of Mr Russell's (the cello teacher) bottom from behind a slipped towel on Hornsea beach. Presumably he would be arrested today. Needless to say the lowlight was the daily rehearsal – it was something of a challenge to appear to be playing the violin without making a noise!

The thing was, I had to remain miserable as a matter of principle but the longer the 'holiday' went on the harder it got. I can't say even now that I had a brilliant time but I think I probably had a better time over those days/weeks/months than I will ever admit to.

The dormitory seemed very long, with beds down each side. It was the first time I'd seen a dormitory. My friends and I picked beds at the top end. There was a room at the bottom end for the teacher. I felt safe knowing she'd be there. It was the first time I'd ever been away from home on my own. After being there a few nights, a few of us decided to have a midnight feast after lights out, we got together and ate biscuits and sweets, we thought it was great.

We had a nice day out at Hornsea Mere. We went out on a boat. There were swans and ducks with their babies. I seem to remember getting my feet wet. We were kept busy, and I never got bored or wanted to come home. My holiday was great fun, giving me a wonderful opportunity to mix with my friends. I look back now knowing it was one of my happiest times. It must have been hard work for the teacher and everyone concerned, and I am truly grateful.

I went to Hornsea on two or three occasions: I loved it every time I went. My only claim to fame at that time was when I got the slipper from our teacher who became a famous writer, Mr David Storey. He wrote the book *This Sporting Life*. Mr Storey was a relief teacher at Ings Road at the time.

Our beds were the old camp beds with a small wooden locker by the side, we used to rise each day at seven, race across to the ablutions block to wash and clean our teeth. Then to a good healthy breakfast of cereals or porridge for starters. We had to keep our beds and the dormitory clean and tidy. Our spending money was put into a day bank run by a teacher. So each day at a certain time we could draw out what we needed. If we went to Hornsea in school term, lessons were introduced.

Evenings we had board games, sing songs, some girls even put on a show to entertain us. Then it was supper time when we usually had a cup of milk and bread with dripping on. Then a good wash or shower. There was always a teacher on hand to make sure there was no fooling round. Then to bed. All this just for thirty shillings.

One Warden could spot a child with dirt on his shoes and going into his beloved classroom at 100 yards. We knew this but what the Warden didn't know was that within four hours of our arrival there would be strings in all directions pinned across his ceiling with dripping batik hanging and releasing copious amounts of all colours of dye onto paper on his precious polished floor. Even worse, every sink had been commandeered and was full of vile coloured liquid. Just as disastrous, every bench was covered with stones and glue (on paper). Having created what must have looked like a scene of devastation, it gave us satisfaction to see the apoplectic look on the Warden's face whilst his eyes seemed to stick out like organ stops. By the end of the week the room was back in pristine condition and the children still treasure their batik and pebble work.

After an exciting day out conversation between 40+ children can quickly erupt to quite a crescendo. This has never been popular with Wardens who are apt to complain about noise levels and children not sitting properly on their chairs. One particular school was prone to bring a very large case of homemade wine which they could enjoy with their tea. The problem arose when the Warden decided to stay for tea. Not being sure how long the wine drinking would be accepted, when asked, the reply was that it was a superb kind of Ribena. Two glasses later we heard a loud crash, a chair spinning across the Dining Hall and a Warden sprawled on the floor chuckling. The blackberry wine was rather potent but for the rest of the week we had a happy and very helpful warden.

Before going to Hornsea we took a form home to our parents to fill in. Various questions had to be answered in regards to our health. We then had a medical. We were then weighed and this was recorded. Also Mrs Patterson, Matron at Hornsea, weighed us when we came home to see how much weight we had gained. What a lovely and enjoyable time I had all for the cost of thirty shilling for three weeks. I enjoyed it so much as I had never had a holiday in my life before.

Times were hard for Mum, Dad being away in the army. Dad would save his army rations of chocolate up for us when he came on leave. We did appreciate everything. Cousin May used to knit for us. Auntie used to give us homemade jam and any baking she had left. There was no such thing as pocket money. To go to the cinema we collected empty jam jars or took pop bottles back for a few coppers. We sang carols for money so Mum could buy us extra food.

It was the year 1948 when at thirteen years of age I went for a three week stay at the Seaside School. I was in Hornsea Dormitory, a teacher was in charge and slept in a room just off ours. Meals were excellent and after all the fresh air during the day, we certainly looked forward to them. The day used to start about 7am with Wash and Brush Up then over to the dining room for a breakfast usually starting with porridge. Although it was lumpy sometimes, I enjoyed it. I went in school time so we had a few lessons to do.

We enjoyed the day's activities. We looked forward to the evenings having concerts, playing draughts, reading, writing our letters for home. Then after, a wash and bath with a teacher watching over us, we rushed over to the dining hall for our slice of dripping and bread and a beaker of milk. Following that we rushed over to our dormitories to share our goodies that we'd bought during the day. Then we listened to ghost stories we made up and what the blue light in the centre of the dormitory created in our memories was nobody's guess.

I went to Hornsea Seaside School in September 1947, my first holiday away from home, and couldn't wait to get away. My elder sister, Irene, ruled the roost a bit and was always ordering me around. I attended Snapethorpe School on the Lupset Estate and was very excited at the opportunity. It was a big thing for me to go anywhere on my own. I had a good friend, who made excuses for us to go out after school. We shared the Hornsea dormitory at Hornsea and although we had our form teacher with us we enjoyed it very much. Mrs Imber, our class teacher, was very strict at school, but mellowed and we all became friends on holiday. We all did our lessons first thing after breakfast, which was a treat, getting anything other than toast, a meat and potato pie for dinner and rice pudding was a nice change. We were allowed to go down to the village shop in the afternoon to spend our sweet coupons on little treats. We went on lovely nature walks and wrote compositions of our exploits when we got back. Our family came to see us at the weekends, which upset some of the girls. One in particular sat up all night crying to go home. All in all it was a happy time, and holds many happy memories.

I can remember clearly a teacher from school, Miss Dews, she was our General Education teacher and was a big influence on me. She was strict, but very clever, and I remember once she said to me, 'In this life, when you go out into the world, try and not be an also ran, try always to be in the first three.'

When I was at school I bought my first camera. Years later I joined the Royal Photographic Society and eventually became a fellow. This is as high as I could get. When I reached that achievement, I thought back to the words of Miss Dews.

Hornsea School was my first ever time away from my parents. The first thing we did when we got there was to go to the beach, I thought, 'This isn't a bit like school.' Because we were art students we were taken to do a lot of drawings. It was the first time I ever went to North Landing in Flamborough, it was beautiful, we sat down and drew the cliffs, I found them totally fascinating.

I took some of my first ever photos on that trip. I still have the negatives to this day. I had a little box camera and it was amazing to have so many subjects to photograph.

I came home from Hornsea on 29th May, 1953, only a couple of days before the Coronation. I had a chance to go back the following year, but it was around Easter time and I was coming up to school leaving age. I decided to take a job at a printers. Most of the others had two weeks off that Easter and some went back to Hornsea. I had two days off and started my working life.

CHAPTER SEVEN
WAKEFIELD ON SEA

The seaside school reopened in 1939, with Miss Hawkins returning as Teacher-in-Charge with the girls, who had the first half of the season, and another Cathedral Boys' schoolmaster, Mr J. Thompson, with the boys. The first season's caretakers, Mr and Mrs Beverley, had clearly found the experience too much for them, as they resigned at the end of January 1939, but replacements were quickly found. The Education Committee rather belatedly realised that having a school on a large field meant that sooner or later the grass would have to be cut, and as late as 20th June authorised the employment of 'a man in connection with scything the grass', and also the purchase of a lawn mower. Even in July, with war looming, the Committee was still looking for volunteers to work on the 'holiday camp' part of the season in August: and in fact the holiday for 'necessitous' children did take place. But the period of the boys' residence was curtailed: the seaside school closed on 28th August, 1939, and would not be used again by Wakefield children for nearly eight years. The blankets used at the school were withdrawn and loaned to the Public Assistance Committee, the caretaker and cook were put on their Winter retainer and the matron reported for duty in Wakefield, being employed by the School Medical Service as a clinic nurse. The buildings then stood empty for some months: they were not finally requisitioned until May 1940, putting an end to the debates about their use which surface in the Education Committee's minutes over the Winter of 1939/40. Hull Trinity House couldn't afford the rent demanded by Wakefield; and councillors also considered a request from the Port of Hull Sailors Orphan Homes Society for use during July and from the East Riding County Council for use 'in connection with the prevention and relief of distress in the event of air raids'. The school once requisitioned was used as a billeting centre for officers; the Council enquired in November 1944 about the possibility of derequisitioning, but was rebuffed, and it was not until August 1945 that it was possible for the Chairman of the Education Committee and his Deputy, with the Director of Education, to visit the school. They reported to the Elementary Education Sub-Committee on 10th September, 1945, that they were 'disturbed at the neglected condition of the school', and the Council agreed to press again for early derequisitioning. This appears to have been conceded by the War Office late in 1945 or early in 1946, and the City Surveyor was instructed to prepare claims for the cost of making good the premises. Another sign of normality returning was the reconstitution on 11th March, 1946, of the Seaside School Sub-Committee. The War Department, after some negotiation, eventually agreed a reinstatement claim of £1588/17/11 plus £43/15/0 'quasi rent', though not until November 1946. This sufficed to cover repair costs, but the repairs themselves took time to complete and the members' ambitions to have the school ready for reopening in April 1947 were thwarted. The Council evidently wanted Hornsea to be used much as it had been before the war, including the provision of a holiday camp for 'debilitated children selected by the school medical officer' in July/August; and members also considered the possibility of providing accommodation under canvas for this period to allow the school to be used as a mixed camp and enable more of the 'debilitated' to stay for 4 weeks. Nothing seems to have come of this. A caretaker, cook and matron were appointed by the end of March 1947, but all of them withdrew acceptance of their appointments; the eventual appointment of Mrs Paterson as matron, as late as July 1947, after the salary of the post had been raised from £3 to £3/10/0 per week gave Hornsea one of its 'characters', vividly remembered by many children. (One recalls her as 'smoking like a chimney'.) Mrs Paterson lost one battle early in her appointment: she was clear that the premises could not be ready before 28th July, but the Committee insisted that the school must open on 21st July, 1947, and it apparently did.

Thereafter, the seaside school settled down to a relatively uneventful existence until 1974, when it was taken into the Education Department of the new Wakefield Metropolitan District Council. Visits to Hornsea became part of the annual routine of the secondary modern (later City High) schools and of an increasing number of primary schools. The opportunities offered by the school were still greatly appreciated, as will be seen, but inevitably the sense of Hornsea as something special began to fade. Partly this is to be explained by the death or retirement of those who had the original vision for Hornsea (as long as Berry was Director of Education he evidently retained a particular affection for the school, visiting it regularly and sometimes staying overnight. Alderman Johnson did the same). Their successors were perhaps less sure of the school's rationale in changing times. Of course, as the 1950s and 60s progressed, more children and more families enjoyed greater opportunities for holidays, and in more exotic locations than Hornsea; standards of public health and nutrition improved dramatically; and expectations of entertainment and the use of leisure time changed. Certainly there is little sign that the City Council gave much, if any, thought to how Hornsea might change or develop. There was no restatement of the school's aims and functions, or reflection on its value to support the school curriculum. The Seaside School Sub-Committee and the other committees overseeing the school were content, mostly, to deal with appointments, ideas for reordering the buildings, contracts for transport and the supply of food, and occasionally fighting off requests from outside bodies for the use of the premises. For example, in 1952, they refused to accommodate 'deaf and dumb' children during the Summer vacation 'owing to the difficulties of the age range', and in 1953 declined a request to use it for convalescent treatment. The question of accommodating deaf and dumb boys was raised again in 1954, and the Chairman and Vice-Chairman agreed to interview the 'local superintendent of the deaf and dumb', to learn more about his requirements: but nothing appears to have come of the request, and similarly rejected were requests for Summer use from Nortonthorpe Boys Hostel, Sussex in 1957, and the youth department of the Presbyterian Church of England in 1958. They did allow a group of touring Australian schoolboy rugby league internationals to have use of the school in January 1973, and also permitted stays by residents of children's homes. Hull LEA was allowed to use the school from November 1973 until March 1974 as a sixth form centre.

The original design and layout of the buildings was clearly not satisfactory. The failure to provide for a sick bay (apparently in spite of the promises in the early publicity) and a drying room for wet clothes on the frequent occasions where children (and staff) were caught in heavy showers caused major inconvenience and was not quickly remedied. The teachers accompanying children to the school might also have been annoyed that it took some time to supply hot water to their rooms. Improvements were made, but slowly and usually after prodding from the teacher representatives on the sub-committee. In 1950, and again in 1954, major improvements to the facilities at Hornsea, including two additional dormitories and the provision of covered walkways to the ablutions block were approved, in principle, but the finance couldn't be found. In 1958, the City Engineer warned members that the heating system was in urgent need of replacement: he reminded them that the original installation was only designed to provide background heating in the spring and autumn, and that if use was to be extended then a full upgrade would be required. The Council could not proceed with the full renewal, and the logbooks reveal the discomfort that caused when the season was extended, as will be seen later in this chapter. More renewals were financed when mixed parties started to become the norm, and the kitchens were also modernised in the mid-1960s. An extra classroom was provided after 1974: technically, a 'temporary classroom', and not in the same style as the rest of the buildings, which have retained their 1930s character, it was still there in 1998, and required far more extensive refurbishment than the original accommodation.

For many years the supplementary payments made available to teachers-in-charge at the school were unchanged at £120 per year or £2 per week, with assistant teachers receiving £1 per week. As the years went by, the number of people able and willing to take on the job of, effectively, Headteacher in residence decreased and after late 1955 the appointments lapsed. The summer camps increasingly had to be staffed by students from Bretton Hall, attracted by the offer of an assistant teacher's pay for the duration of the camps, topped up by a £2 per week residential allowance. Teachers also appear to have at least mildly resented the restrictions on their receiving visitors. In 1963 it was noted that each teacher accompanying children to the school could receive two visitors per fortnight (the three-weeks stays having been abandoned): reasonable hospitality could be offered, though permits had to be obtained from the Education Department. By 1970 staffing difficulties extended to the domestic staff, and retainer fees had to be more widely introduced. The school was fortunate during much of the post war period, until 1972, to have had the services of Mrs Nicholson as cook, and later as cook/housekeeper. Her husband had been caretaker, but she had stayed on after his death in 1956, and her personality and catering abilities drew consistent appreciation from the staff and pupils attending the school. After 1959, a matron was not appointed and the medical needs of the school were attended to by Hornsea's GPs.

Each year, hundreds of children made the coach journey from Wakefield to Hornsea, conveyed by Frankish of Brandesburton, or Belle Vue Garage, or Victoria Motors, generally without incident: not every coach suffering delays because of 'an unfortunate incident with a sheep' as St Austin's experienced in September 1954. For a while in the early 1970s, Eastmoor High School dispensed with the normal transport: they had their own bus, and relished the independence that gave them. Usually between seven and 800 children attended, though the numbers increased after the introduction of mixed parties in 1966, the gradual extension of the season into November, the introduction of music courses, and the increased use by primary school children. The practice of three-week stays had largely ceased by 1958, when both boys and girls stayed for a fortnight: since 1953 girls had generally been staying for the shorter period. This created time for wider primary school use. In spite of the staffing difficulties which occasionally meant the cancellation of a visit (as, for example, with St Thomas à Becket's visit in June 1968), a visit to Hornsea was clearly seen as a regular part of most children's education.

Each year, some months before a school was scheduled to go to Hornsea, the Headteacher received a pack of materials from the Education Department - letter to parents and application forms, timetables, clothing lists, copies of Hornsea's rules and consent forms on which parents could specify which church service they wanted their children to attend, and whether they would allow their children to bathe in the sea. These were distributed to whatever year group was allocated time at Hornsea. A set of these documents for 1969 has survived, as they were used as supporting material for a Bretton Hall student's dissertation, which he chose to write on Hornsea. From them we learn that, 37 years after the seaside school opened, the cost of a week's stay at Hornsea had risen to £1/17/6, and that parents were urged not to let their offspring have more than 15/ per week in pocket money, which was to cover not just incidental expenses but also the costs of the excursions to Beverley, Hull and Bridlington, amounting to 6/−. That was generally a vain hope: for all that the Education Committee advised that 'many children take far too much spending money with them', staff noticed that a lot of children took above the recommended amount or had it topped up on parents' weekend. The 'under-privileged children who were kept short of money found it hard to keep pace with the big spenders'. Parents were still assured that the seaside school would 'continue the education of each child...under ideal and health giving conditions', and that 'simple food of the best quality' would be provided. This was to discourage the sending of food parcels to children - a practice deemed 'quite unnecessary'. Parents were enjoined to ensure that no pocket knives of any description were taken to Hornsea, and in a wonderfully grandmotherly conclusion to the letter, parents were told: 'it has been noted that children at Hornsea show great disappointment if they do not receive news from home. This is quite understandable, and all parents will, no doubt, wish to write to their children during their stay'. The children were generally expected to write a letter or postcard home on the first evening of their stay, assuring their parents of their safe arrival. The timetable was much as it had been when the school opened, with the morning bell still sounding at 7am on weekdays and Saturdays, and bedtime drinks served at 8pm or a little later. The Seaside School's rules are a mixture of the obvious: 'walls, furniture, mattresses, pillows, bedlinen...must not be marked or damaged in any way', reflections of problems which would have arisen in the past (like the strict prohibition of knives and water pistols or 'rough play' in the dormitories and the ban on the wearing of football boots in the Hall) and the draconian: 'walking on the lawns is forbidden'. Visitors were not allowed without a permit, except those parents coming to the school on visiting day.

The timetable of course had a strong outdoor bias. During term time, two informal lessons were given each morning. English tended to take the form of keeping a Hornsea diary and corresponding with parents and friends. Mathematics often concentrated on the practical aspects of allocating spending money, auditing personal bank accounts, drawing plans of the school, or marking out sports areas. Geography included studying the route to

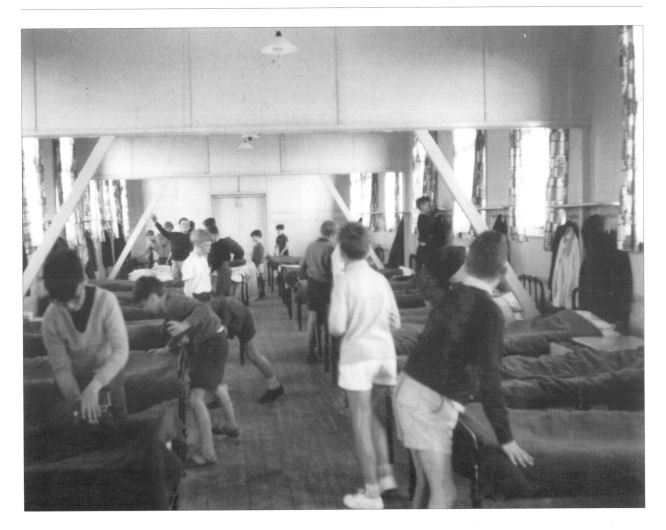

Hornsea, Ordnance Survey maps of the locality, coastal erosion, collections of fossils, navigation by compass, or the weather and cloud formations. Ings Road school broadened their geography studies into full-blown 'adventure courses', where parties left the centre in relays for nights under canvas. History tended to concentrate on the town of Hornsea itself; throughout the 1950s and 60s the Verger of the Parish Church was frequently employed in showing parties of Wakefield visitors round the Church. Few schools enjoyed quite the detailed historical studies of Manygates Secondary Modern in June 1957, when Miss Burnet undertook a series of lessons starting with the 'East Riding pre ice-age', and continued each day through the ice, stone and bronze ages through to the Romans and the Saxons and improved the excursion to Beverley with a description of the different types of architecture to look out for.

The position of the seaside school near to Hornsea Mere and the coast gave ample opportunities for nature study. A group from St Austin's Upper School and Ings Road in September 1948 visited a local gamekeeper 'and were given a thorough explanation of many interesting points in his life'; and a group of St Austin's girls visited in September 1949 to inspect his dogs, ferrets and pigs and learn about the open and close seasons for shooting. A lecture on the Mere by 'Mr Oliver, the Hornsea antiquarian', was 'very much appreciated' by boys from Manygates in April 1949. But nature study was more often conducted by direct observation. This could sometimes be extremely detailed: a party of Cathedral School boys in May 1949 'journeyed along the Hull Road to 'examine...the construction of a buttercup', and the same group spent time on the sands 'examining how to drain wet surfaces...how rivers worked and how deltas are produced'. More often, though, nature rambles were preferred, often for the purpose of collecting specimens for mounting and display, or for drawing later: St John's Girls' School especially liked to gather flowers for pressing, or for making posies. A group from the Art School visiting in October 1951 put their ramble to good use by collecting sufficient blackberries to make tarts for lunch: but for many pupils, the Mere and the seashore opened their eyes to the richness of bird and plant life; and to judge from the number of fossils collected down the years it is surprising that any remain to be discovered by succeeding generations. Wardens of the bird sanctuary established on the Mere have frequently given of their time to describe their work: and the log books kept at the school from 1948-1974 often reveal the simple pleasure city children obtained from being in the fresh air. Nature occasionally disconcerted them: a herd of bullocks frightened a party of girls from St Thomas à Becket in 1964; and Jennifer Laverack of St. John's was stung by a jellyfish in June 1966 and had to be taken to hospital. The walk round the Mere was demanding for the younger children: it was recorded of Heath View girls in 1961 that they were 'very game, but their legs are short...'. The Mere was sometimes visited less energetically, through tours on a motor launch: though some schools undertook the 'great adventure' of sailing. Occasionally the visitors got into trouble with the local farmers, as in June 1960 when some 'over enthusiastic' girls from Manygates, taking part in a 'grand scrounge' raided a field of sheep for a piece of wool. For the most part, the encounter with the natural world was a happy one. Lawefield Lane's junior girls in 1960 found 'the trees at their best...we enjoyed it thoroughly', and 'they were delighted to find a donkey and a friendly cat' (which the teacher in charge, Mrs Cooper, christened Muriel) on their farm walk. As late as 1966, Hornsea was still welcoming pupils who had not seen the sea. Two boys from Ings Road High School were induced to paddle 'and the way they reacted was marvellous to see'. Hornsea was not the only piece of coastline visited: most parties explored Flamborough Head and North Landing, and some took the chance of serious bird watching: and the girls of Ings Road in July 1964 were 'fascinated and exhilarated' by their exploration of the sea life on Filey Brig: 'hordes of starfish of all colours of orange and pink, hermit crabs, sea anemones...'.

In most stays, there were usually two or three excursions out of Hornsea, to Hull, Beverley and Filey/Bridlington and Flamborough Head, which were in general calculated to combine instruction and amusement (Bridlington was mostly for souvenir hunting). In Beverley, the focus of attention tended to be the Minster, St Mary's Church, and the shipyards, which then carried on a flourishing trade in building trawlers. Many Wakefield parties no doubt emulated the 'reverent interest' in the Minster boys from Lawefield Lane and the Art School are recorded as showing in June 1954: and Manygates boys in 1964 'enthusiastically received' the Verger's talk. The stocks, pillory and other ancient relics in the Flemish Weavers Room at St Mary's particularly excited a number of Ings Road boys in August that year. In July 1959, a party of girls from Ings Road and Lawefield Lane ventured up the Minster tower: Mrs Cooper, in charge of the party, recorded that 'I was not alone in suffering from acute claustrophobia in the narrow, airless staircase. Several girls were in tears when they reached the top: the view was magnificent, but we were nervous of the descent and most of us did it in bare or stockinged feet'. In spite of that, 'we all put something into the collection'. Many of the trips to Hull were for sport: parties of boys sometimes were taken to watch soccer, or Rugby League matches, especially if Wakefield Trinity was playing, and children staying at Hornsea sometimes took part in swimming galas in Hull, winning a number of prizes. But in the 1950s especially, a highlight of a tour of Hull docks was the chance to go round a liner berthed there, or it might be a cargo ship or a troopship. The Wilberforce Museum was a popular trip; Ings Road girls in July 1949 were 'entranced' by the exhibits. Inevitably fish were a feature of trips to Hull. Visits to the fish dock occasioned complaints about the smell, though the gift of 80 cod fillets received by St John's girls in 1961 was very welcome and in May 1965 those Cathedral and Methodist school boys who visited the Ross Frozen fish factory found their experience just as rewarding as did those members of the party who went to inspect the Lightning Jets at RAF Leconfield. In June 1969, the Cathedral schoolgirls were honest enough to record that they visited Hull 'to look round the shops'. But trips to Hull weren't without their problems. In October 1966, Snapethorpe City High School found that 'Ladies conveniences were like water in the desert …'. Snapethorpe was not alone. In May 1974, Lawefield Middle School had an eventful visit to Hull, where after lunch in East Park, 'a minor disaster occurred, owing to a shortage of toilets and toilet paper in the right places!' That visit was, however, redeemed by a chance encounter with one J H Green, 86 years old, and the last survivor of Shackleton's Antarctic Expedition, and by successful museum visits, with the guide at the Transport Museum being 'most attentive and helpful, especially to the female staff'.

Then as now, the trip to Flamborough Head provided enormous pleasure. In July 1959, the trip by Ings Road/Lawefield Lane was described as 'a lovely day in every respect. The walk...over the cliffs was delightful...at North Landing we went for a sail round the coves. The water is incredibly clear, the sand like birdseed, and the birds on the cliffs provided yet another pleasure. We saw cormorants, puffins, gulls of all kinds. We went into the smugglers' cave. All for 1/- each!'. The same combination of schools in May 1960 had a serendipitous encounter at North Landing with a Wakefield couple, Mr & Mrs Andrassy, whose 'wicked, ugly, very intelligent mongrel', called Richard, 'with more than its share of personal charm', played with the girls, causing 'quite a circus'. The Andrassys cemented their popularity by paying for tea for the 18 girls and the staff. Apart from the bird life, visits to North Landing were occasionally enlivened by seeing lifeboat practices, and it was sometimes possible to ascend the Flamborough Lighthouse, though this often depended on the keeper being in a good mood. Bridlington was ideal for souvenir hunting and the amusement arcades. Visits to Butlins camp at Filey were rare, though St John's girls went in 1969. In 1964, Manygates boys, on a trip to Scarborough, were 'interested to see Freddie Trueman unsuccessfully trying to introduce his daughter to exercising on the trampoline'. The great man was later invited to visit Hornsea but declined, apparently rather emphatically, having been roused from slumber to receive the invitation by telephone. The variety of excursions grew as the years passed. Flamingo Park became a frequent destination, and there were the occasional visits to Sewerby Park, Burton Agnes Hall (where, as Belle Vue School was told in September 1972, the real Blue Lady lived), and Burton Constable. In 1974, Manygates Middle School showed 'quite a genuine interest in the Hall itself, more when they realised there was a café and even more on discovering the playground'. In March 1976, Stanley Grove J I (one of the first non-Wakefield City Schools to visit after local government reorganisation created a much larger Wakefield LEA), ambitiously visited Wharram Percy, the unique deserted Medieval Village: 'after extensive preparation and research, what did the kids do? Did they look for specific sites? Did they look for field systems? Did they sit quietly and absorb the peace and atmosphere? Oh no: they rolled down the hill time and time again. A wonderful experience in centrifugal force, but one which could have been done in Stanley on the slag heaps'.

Of course, no trip to Hornsea would have been complete without a visit to the Pottery. Children at the Seaside school visited the Pottery both to see objects being made, and to buy small souvenirs to take home. For some years there were two visits: one to reserve gifts and a second to collect them. As with all the excursions away from the school itself the log book betrays some anxiety on the part of the teachers about the potential and actual behaviour of the children (and relief when things didn't go wrong) but often the Pottery trips were highlights of the stay in Hornsea and were encouraged by the owners. For the visit of girls from Ings Road and Sandal Magna Junior School in May 1962, the 'people at the Potteries were very kind and patient with the children, and reduced many of the articles on sale just for them'. The next visitors, girls from the Cathedral School also found the pottery guides 'interesting and instructive'. By 1963, however, the same school found the variety of pottery on display 'disappointing'. The Pottery had begun to charge for visits, but this was waived for the Wakefield visitors. Hornsea Potteries retained Wakefield's loyalties, in spite of the appearance of a rival concern at Ulrome, offering 'pieces which the children can easily afford'. The log books note the gradual extension of the Potteries and the development of other attractions on the site, to the extent that one school is recorded as enjoying the animals and birds more than the factory itself: Park School in September 1974 especially favoured the 'bumping cars' and the climbing frame. The facilities, like the adventure playground and the managerie, provided a respite for teachers looking to divert the children. When Lawefield Lane and St Mary's visited in October 1973, one child 'entertained the monkeys, who seemed appreciative at first, but we were soon thankful of the double wire netting of the cages, as they began to throw themselves about in a most vigorous manner'.

The town of Hornsea itself was of course frequently and extensively visited for shopping, swimming, entertainment and study. For a long time, school visits to the town, for whatever purpose, were formal affairs, with the children marching to town or beach in a crocodile, wearing uniforms. Over the years, local people will have got used to parties of

Wakefield children sketching the Parish Church, (as well as attending it in substantial numbers), going on treasure hunts around the town, producing guides to Hornsea, and doing odd projects like studying the variety of road signs to be found there. For some years, certainly into the 1960s, visiting parties used to play cricket and football matches against Hornsea School, or against the Hornsea Youth Club (against which St Austin's recorded 'a grand game and a great victory'). Girls from the Cathedral School in 1972 had a more social encounter with Hornsea School: 'after a chance meeting with Fifth Year boys of Hornsea School at the Mere, and them rescuing several damsels in distress...after a good deal of deliberation...we decided to invite them to a 'Disco' on Saturday evening. The girls embarked on preparation as a project and spent all day...preparing. A member of their staff accompanied them, which gave them a chance to meet each other under controlled circumstances'. Concerts at the conclusion of the music courses which were a regular feature of the use of the school from the late 1960s onwards, were given at Hornsea School, as well as at 'The Willows' old folks home, and on 31 August, 1972 at the Floral Hall, when the Youth Chamber Orchestra performed (and felt that their efforts were 'well appreciated' by the local residents). As the original hope, that residents at the seaside school would make their own entertainment in the evenings, began to be diluted, so Hornsea's Star Cinema began to be frequented regularly, and films such as *Captain Horatio Hornblower*, *Moby Dick*, *Quo Vadis* and *The Yangtse Incident* were apparently greatly enjoyed. *Spartacus* is reported to have reduced Ings Road girls to tears when they saw it in July 1963. The shows put on at the Floral Hall were often visited, including *The Quaker Girl*, *The Desert Song*, *Oklahoma* and *The Mikado*, and a party from St Thomas à Becket was no doubt pleased to get a concessionary price of 1/- a head for performances of *The Brides of Seville*, a children's version of Rossini's *Barber of Seville* when it was produced in April 1965. Manygates boys attended a 'Dance to the Top 20' at the Floral Hall in September 1962, where a 'really good twisting time was apparently thoroughly enjoyed' ('Chacun à son goût' was the comment of the teacher in charge, Mr Sutcliffe). Rather less successful was the trip by Cathedral girls to a Beat Group competition in the Floral Hall in July 1965: there was no competition as only one group turned up. A music course in April 1970 had a more obviously cultural outing, travelling to Hull to see *Rigoletto* at the New Theatre, an experience which turned them all into 'confirmed opera fans'.

The Wakefield children seem to have joined in local events quite freely: Cathedral School boys were among those to go down to the beach on 19 June, 1953 to see the Destroyer 'Duchess' visiting as part of the Coronation celebrations, and over the years, the school's weekends were enlivened by visits to the Hornsea carnival. Snapethorpe girls attended the crowning of the Carnival Queen in 1952; in August 1962 the Junior School holiday group went to the beach to see the 'gala of boats', and the selection of 'Miss Mermaid'; and in August 1965 Ings Road girls were no doubt diverted by the 'mock invasion' of the beach by the Hornsea Boat Club, the boats decorated as 'a Viking Armada'. In 1968 the Carnival's fancy dress parade with 'ingenious costumes' provided Cathedral girls with 'much entertainment'. A slightly more gruesome activity was arranged in August 1959 when a party of girls were used in a civil defence exercise in Beverley. They provided 'very realistic casualties'. The beach and the sea front of course provided a focus for the school's activities. There were hazards: a small unexploded bomb was found on the beach in April 1957 and the occasional incident of children being stung by jellyfish is recorded. The need to take care to avoid swimming near the sewage outfall pipe is also mentioned: a crack in the pipe stopped Manygates boys taking a swim in July 1965 and there was still a problem in September 1973 when Lawefield Junior School children, 'unabashed...swam alongside the sewage pipe, and showers were a must that night'. Some schools clearly failed to study the tide tables. Stanley Grove in March 1976 were disconcerted to find that 'the sea had suddenly receded: I didn't know Moses or Canute was in the party'. The beach was also the scene of a display of heroism by a Wakefield teacher: on 1 September, 1958, while St Austin's boys were swimming, the SOS alarm was raised, and Christopher Rayner, a student teacher, 'stripped, entered the water, and rescued a twelve year old boy, David Johnson of Cottingham, from drowning. The boy was only semi-conscious when Mr Rayner brought him out of the sea'. The log book entry concealed the fact that Mr Rayner was only 19 at the time, and had to swim above a half a mile to effect the rescue. Mr. Rayner later received the Royal Humane Society's certificate on vellum from the Mayor at a ceremony in Wakefield Town Hall.

But such incidents were happily rare: and Wakefield children were able to make full use of the beach and its associated facilities. Apart from swimming (or dodging the waves breaking on the beach or the promenade on breezy days), there were regular sandcastle building competitions, sometimes judged by interested passers by. The amusement arcades attracted much attention: Mr. Greenwood of Crofton, who visited with Manygates in 1948, recalls that he and his friends spent much of their pocket money there on the juke boxes to play 'Near You', the hit song of the time. The boating lake was also popular, for releasing high spirits apart from any other purpose: on 1 April, 1963 Cathedral School boys 'attracted a great number of spectators by their antics' there. No doubt similar attention was paid to the Ings Road girls discovered 'ankle deep in shrimp bits' outside the Parish Church in July 1959 after a morning shopping in Hornsea, but the teachers made them pick every bit of debris up and deposit them in the waste bin. Teachers themselves caused something of a spectacle in September 1974, when Mr Stephenson and Miss Barker from Belle Vue School took the children's clothes to the launderette, and over-soaped the machines, having, therefore, to spend half an hour 'collecting suds in any available receptacle and depositing them in the main street of Hornsea'.

The Seaside School and its children were most obviously on display on Sunday mornings: on most Sundays from the 1947 reopening up to the early 1970s, formal church parade was insisted on, and parties went, willingly or not, to the churches in town. The Roman Catholics often went twice: to mass and Benediction (in September 1964, the 'lovely singing' of the girls of St Thomas à Becket at the latter office caused particular comment). The Protestant children usually only attended once, but the CE Schools, Cathedral and St John's also sometimes observed major feasts and patronal festivals. The churches seem to have tried to welcome the Wakefield parties and the clergy made some effort to extend pastoral care to the school. One of the Methodist clergy, a Mr F. Humble, went so far as to write to the

Education Committee in 1955 saying 'that he had visited the Seaside School, stating how delighted he was with everything he saw, and hoping he would be allowed to visit from time to time'. The Committee made no comment. The Church of England seems to have disconcerted the children and teachers by progressively dropping Mattins in favour of Parish Communion services, whose length and content were felt to be unsuitable and generally, those who went to the Methodist and the Congregational churches enjoyed themselves more, by reason of the greater opportunity for lusty singing. Church going was an accepted part of the Hornsea visit: the log book only infrequently admits to any coercion of unwilling attenders. Manygates in June 1964 bundled the whole school off to Evensong, 'the three who professed another faith being unable to recall when they last attended their place of worship'; twelve years on, Stanley Grove J I also took the children to church... 'all C of E. Fortunately we quelled the natural desires of our Moslem and Sikh brothers explaining that the experience would be beneficial, comparative religions, etc...' The children seem to have coped admirably with what would have been an increasingly alien experience: there are several references in the log books to teachers receiving compliments on their pupils' good behaviour. As the Stanley Grove teacher remarked, 'isn't it nice when you are complimented on the behaviour of your charges. It's a pity people don't realise what you have to do to get them like that'. Sometimes, however the experience of Sunday worship was too much for all parties, as in September 1973, when Belle Vue went to morning service:

'Another visit to church where some audience participation was involved. The Minister held up a piece of Laburnum and asked if anyone could identify it. A confident cry from... in the gallery: 'a bluebell sir'. On being asked to look carefully at the colour, he replied equally confidently 'a yeller bell then'. The group proved to be in good voice for the Lords Prayer, which was sung to the school tune. Unfortunately, the congregation and organist cannot have practised as much as us and ended five bars after us. We are still wondering why we were told we could leave after the third hymn.'

If the welcome pupils at the school received in Hornsea was generally warm, as the years went by there were some disagreeable incidents: the occasional trespasser on the school site, and once in 1963 an intruder in the Hornsea dormitory. In July 1965, Cathedral School girls were disturbed while undressing, and in September 1966, boys known to the Police for making nuisances of themselves 'were seen loitering on the school field' while the same school was taking evening showers. Another group of boys in July 1968 followed Cathedral School girls back from a dance at the Floral Hall: in the same year 'local youths' caused trouble with a group on the Primary school holiday visit. More seriously, in 1971, 'the Mereside Boot Boys', conducted a sort of guerilla war against the instrumental course in residence in April. They tried to pick fights with course members and 'molested' one boy in the town, helpfully informing him that they would be arriving at the school at 7.30pm to 'set about' the older boys. Nine boot boys 'attacked the school', but were foiled by the Police, assisted by the course director, Mr Davies, and pupils.

Some of the visiting groups misbehaved, of course, and the prevailing air of good behaviour among the Wakefield children was sometimes called in question, though mostly the children adapted well to communal life. Petty theft and shoplifting are noted in the log books, especially when the children were let off the leash in Bridlington or given free time in Hornsea itself. The attempts at thieving were often amateurish (as the teachers at Stanley Grove noted with exasperation in 1976 'if they are going to steal, why at least can't they be intelligent about it?') but the Police were usually called to deal with the troublemakers and cautioned them. The staff accompanying the visits were firm with 'anti-social behaviour', and one entry speaks of boys being 'chastised' for misdemeanours on one of the music courses. The chastisement, presumably, wasn't merely verbal. There were some cases of damage to the school, like the graffiti left behind by Manygates girls in 1961, and the staff of some schools evidently had good cause to be vigilant. Mr Fricker of Snapethorpe Secondary School confiscated 10 knives on 13 October, 1961 and the following night organised a search of the dormitories for cigarettes. Staff emphasised the 'importance of outdoor behaviour', 'manners' and 'cleanliness and honesty' in their introductory talks, and found that the emphasis on the daily inspection of 'kit and person' was 'extremely helpful in maintaining discipline'. The combination of plentiful food and frequent exercise helped to tire the children out and get them ready for bed, but if they refused to settle down, there was always the sanction of late night physical education, as applied to Manygates girls in July 1958. The introduction of mixed parties raised the possibility of other hazards: Stanley Grove staff were probably not alone in 'foiling amorous exploits', or as they were honest enough to admit 'we think most were foiled'. In 1967, one of the student helpers on the Summer camps noted that 'love affairs' precipitated moodiness and jealous rivalry amongst a small group of children, though in the following year he noted that 'relationship' were less intense, 'and couples would change about almost daily'.

A feature of the two and three week stays at Hornsea was the parents' visit on the second Sunday. Initially, the parents were ferried in coaches to Hornsea, and the children met them in the town after lunch. They spent the afternoon together, and returned to the school in the early evening to allow the parents to inspect the accommodation and see a little of the work that their children had been doing. Some schools made a particular effort to decorate the classrooms for parents' day, and to display work attractively. After the tour of the school, the parents were returned to Wakefield. The log books suggest that the visit, though eagerly anticipated, not least for the possibility of topping up pocket money, was not infrequently unsettling. Those children who for whatever reason had no visitors were very much in the minority and had to be specially catered for; sometimes parents who were expected failed to turn up, or were late, and the children's distress and anxiety were painful for the staff; and parental visits often triggered homesickness, especially among the younger children, and bags had to be packed hastily to allow them to travel home on the buses. Even if the children didn't go home prematurely, it was often noted that some were tearful after the parents left. As the years went by, and more parents had their own transport, they seem to have been increasingly unwilling to be confined to the timetable for visiting day laid down by the Education Committee, and demanded earlier access to their offspring, disrupting the school's routine, in spite of stout resistance by the teachers in charge. In 1961, the Education Committee, following a complaint from St John's Girls School, was moved to issue a formal reminder to parents that they were not allowed on the premises before 1.30pm or after 6.30pm. The attitude of parents towards the school and the teachers also seemed to have become more critical, or at least less deferential, with the passing years. In 1948, St Austin's parents were 'expressing their appreciation of all that is being done for their children', and in the mid – 1950s, Manygates and Methodist School's parents are recorded as being 'very pleased with the health and appearance of the boys', or expressing 'pleasure at both the buildings and the fitness of the girls'. In July 1961, the parents of a girl on a St John's visit, removed her from Hornsea, 'objecting to her being chastised for disobedience'. Also in July 1961, Mrs Cooper, in charge of the visit by Ings Road and Heath View girls, whose lengthy log book entries give a superb insight into the life and conduct of the school, noted that of the eight girls who left on parents' day, only one had shown any sign of homesickness, and that 'I honestly believe that each of these girls would have continued to benefit from the school had she remained here, and that had there been no visit, each would have remained. (A stay at Hornsea) is a splendid opportunity for them to live together and work together, and obviously some find it easier than do others, but I feel that those who most needed this opportunity were the ones who were taken away'. Still, Mrs Cooper noted that 'none of the parents had any grumbles, and many came to express their appreciation of the job the school does'. On 9th August 1964, parents' day became heated. On the return to school in the evening:

'The expected tears began to fall. Parents asked for cases and belongings, and the expected exodus began, that is, until permission to take the children was refused. The children admitted to their parents that they were enjoying themselves and were not homesick, so there was no reason to let them go. It was pointed out that the holiday period was for two weeks, not one. One parent began to gather a crowd to go to the Director and ask why, when children had been allowed to go home on visiting Sunday (in) past...years, they were not allowed to do so this week. When he had the support of eight or nine parents, he was emphatically urged to go to the Director the next day, whereupon his supportors sidled away, rather deflated'.

Eventually, three children left, one amid accusations from mother that the dormitory

teacher had opened and read the child's letters before giving them to her. Further disputes occurred the following year. In July 1965 when Cathedral School girls were in residence, it was recorded that:

"Mrs ...... (Christine's mother) went to Mrs Lambert and in a very loud voice and aggressive manner announced that she was taking Christine home...Mrs Lambert protested because the change of activities and freedom from an over-emotional atmosphere is doing Christine a great deal of good. Eventually Christine told her mother that she wanted to stay, and after haranguing a small crowd, Mrs ...... left in tears'.

A couple of weeks later, on the first Sunday of the Primary school girls visit, the parents of one child met the party on the way to church, and insisted that their daughter be allowed to return to Wakefield. The teacher in charge protested, but the parents were not to be denied - they were missing their daughter. On the following Primary boys' visit, another mother 'seemed convinced that her son was homesick, and, almost to the point of rudeness insisted that he should accompany her home'. In August 1968 there were further examples of parents asking their children to go home.

Towards the end of the 1960s and into the 1970s, the increasing number of weeklong visits meant that visiting day became less of a feature of the school's life.

The tensions over discipline, misdemeanours, parents' visits should not of course be overplayed. Most school parties were free of such difficulties, and had happy stays at Hornsea. But many visits inevitably had their share of illnesses and inconveniences, and the matron, and later the Hornsea GPs, notably Doctors French and Ashworth, had to deal with a variety of ailments. Some log book entries read like a succession of medical bulletins. Sometimes the attention paid to the children's well being strikes a modern reader as quaint: in July 1948, the teacher- in-charge of a visit by Manygates boys noted that he 'carried out the usual check on normal functions - nine boys sent for cascara' (a purgative), and there are frequent references to the state of pupils' boils up to the point at which they burst. (The treatment for boils was apparently to apply hot lint to the affected part): and at least one case of scabies was recorded. Some of the ailments were self-inflicted: two boys from Ings

Road in March 1951 reported to matron with sore throats, caused by eating soap, and on one occasion a child had to be rescued from the effects of swallowing buttons. Cases of sleepwalking and nightmares are occasionally recorded: one girl suffered such a succession of nightmares that she had to be sent home, as her classmates were becoming thoroughly frightened.

Some of the outbreaks of sickness were perhaps caused by children becoming over-excited at being away from home: as one teacher from Snapethorpe Middle School commented wearily after what was evidently a hectic week in June 1974, sickness 'was becoming increasingly fashionable'. The custom of telling ghost stories, no doubt featuring the Blue Lady, sometimes affected the impressionable: one boy from St Thomas à Becket suffered convulsions as a result, and one can only speculate on how a broken bottle got into one of the dormitories in June 1960 while Cathedral Girls were in residence: treading on it meant that Judith Batty had to be taken to the Cottage Hospital, which over the years received a steady procession of Wakefield children with appendicitis, and various breaks and sprains. The Hornsea tradition of boisterous games sometimes claimed victims among the staff: a 'rough game of British Bulldog' enjoyed by St Thomas à Becket in April 1966 sent one teacher off to Beverley Hospital with suspected fractured ribs, and a teacher is recorded as having broken a collar bone as a result of exertions during the boys' season in the Spring of 1951. Though at times the staff often worked very long hours and under much pressure, they seem to have coped very well, though in August 1948 one teacher succumbed to a nervous breakdown on a Cathedral/Methodist Boys visit. On two occasions he left the school for lengthy periods without permission, the second time for 10 hours. The Police had to be notified, and when he turned up 'he was unable to give any coherent explanation for his behaviour'. His parents had to take him home.

Usually, the outbreak of illness, if serious for the individual concerned, was confined to one or two children, but sometimes the whole visit was affected. In September 1957, Ings Road girls had a particularly horrendous stay. On the first day, one of the girls swallowed a bee and had to be taken to the doctor; on the third, six girls complained of headaches and sore throats; on the fourth day eight more girls reported similar symptoms; the next day eight more were taken ill - and after a week, 26 girls out of the 37 on the visit, together with the staff, were either suffering, or recovering from, influenza. Not surprisingly, the visit ended prematurely. A visit by Park School also ended suddenly in April 1973, as both staff and pupils developed diarrhoea and vomiting, and a trip by children from St Mary's and Methodist primary schools in 1971 suffered a succession of traumas from a deliberate overdose of tablets through 'hysterical fits' to suspected broken limbs. It rained as well.

Of course, the East Coast weather, though not always good, did sometimes relent sufficiently to allow sunbathing: and 'in spite of all our warnings', that most traditional of seaside ailments, sunburn, resulted. A lot of schools would have welcomed the opportunity to catch the sun, as Hornsea's climate was clearly not consistently idyllic. It could be cold, especially at the beginning and end of each season, ('irritatingly bracing' noted the Music Adviser in April 1972), and the school's buildings were not at first well adapted for such conditions. In 1951, the school opened in March, and the boys in residence complained of the coldness of the dormitories at night. There was also a shortage of coke, and so showers were only possible once every three days. The erratic working of the showers was a fairly frequent irritation. The capacity of the hot water tank was limited anyway, so those who were last into the shower block tended to have a more bracing experience than they expected or desired. Not to have showers at all was a greater problem. Manygates girls' visit in April 1958 was particularly affected. First there were no showers because of a burst pipe in the hot water system, and having been restored, the showers ceased a couple of days later because of another coke shortage. In April 1966, having battled through a snowstorm to reach Hornsea, (the sea front had 'a look of Alaska') Thomas à Becket boys found the showers were out of action because of a faulty mixer valve. After a couple of days the boys were admitted to the converted girls' shower block 'for a much needed shower. Pleasure was soon curtailed when most of the wall tiles fell off after a few minutes contact with the water. A very tired and cold school had an early night in the only warm place - bed'. (This visit was full of incident. A trip round the Mere was notable for the fact that

'Peter Farrell liked the water so much that he decided to swim - fully clothed'. Thomas à Becket appears to have favoured a form of muscular Christianity at this stage of its history, and the visit was packed with cross country runs, two rugby matches and lots of football and cricket - and a catalogue of accompanying minor injuries. But they had a "thoroughly enjoyable" stay!)

There are signs that the condition of the school and its facilities may have been allowed to run down towards the end of its time in the care of Wakefield City LEA: there are frequent notes about the TV and the record player not working properly, and the inadequacy of the heating system. In May 1972, the leader of one of the music courses noted that 'the heating system is fully extended, but did not always rise to the challenge', before noting wistfully, 'perhaps Hornsea does see some good weather, sometimes'. And the showers continued to play up, which meant the girls sometimes having to use the boys' showers because theirs were out of order, much to the confusion of one boy from Lawefield Lane who wandered in while the girls were in occupation. The experience 'completed his education'.

The daily routine could often be altered by more or less pleasant or interesting incidents. From time to time 'The Committee' descended for an inspection of their distant enclave, sometimes meeting representatives of the Hornsea UDC. These visits were the occasion of some civic self-congratulation. In 1957, the Education Committee met at Hornsea and were doubtless pleased by the Chairman of Hornsea UDC's congratulations to Wakefield on 'building such a nice school in pleasant and healthy surroundings'. The need to provide lunch for the visitors affected the school in residence. On 29 June, 1964, Manygates noted rather sniffily: 'we are to dine early to accommodate 'The Committee' who we understand are coming to inspect. We feel we should have been notified officially or asked to suggest a suitable day for the visit which would not interfere with our schedule of work'. And Manygates were not able to evade the Councillors: 'on arrival we are invited to address the Committee and their guests on our work at Hornsea. Interest shown after lunch in the painting, sketching, spinning and survey projects in particular....' Less formal, but rather more frequent, were the visits paid by the Director of Education and Alderman Johnson and

Borkwood on a semi-social basis: it seems as though Hornsea was on occasions used as a weekend retreat or holiday home. For example, in 1948, the Director brought his family for the weekend, and on 12 August, 1951, the teacher in charge noted that 'The Mayor and Mayoress arrived, and will be in residence for a few days'. HMI visited frequently in the years after World War Two: in June 1952, no less than three descended. These visits, though no doubt taken seriously, were evidently less terrifying than an OFSTED inspection nowadays. In 1949, the visiting HMI is recorded as bringing his sister with him; and in 1959, the Inspector found everything in order 'except the previous lack of care of the PE stock'. There was a steady trickle of other official visitors. On 29 June, 1949, the school received '40 women teachers of the Hull Nursery Association'; representatives of the Central Council for Physical Recreation came in July 1954, a party from Mauritius visited in June 1963, and in 1972, Malcolm Gray, the last Director of Education for Wakefield City, visited one of the orchestral courses, bringing with him a Mr R. S. Harrison, 'Deputy Head of a large ILEA comprehensive. Harrison, as an outside guest, seemed very impressed.' Regular visitors in the Summer from 1951 onwards were the members of the Youth Exchange party from Castrop-Rauxel who, often accompanied by the full panoply of a civic retinue, and sometimes in national dress, used Hornsea as their lunch stop en route to Bridlington. For the 1961 visit, while Heath View and Ings Road girls were in residence, Mrs Cooper recorded 'I must say we were rather proud of our girls, they all looked so happy, healthy and well turned out. Mrs Nicholson had provided, as always, a first class meal, which was enjoyed by all. The German party showed its appreciation by singing a song for us, and we replied with a curious but enthusiastic rendering of 'Ilkley Moor baht 'at'. The party ended on a very joyous note...all the Germans were impressed by the school - their leader remarked that it was just what they needed at home, and that they hoped to arrange country schools for their own children'. Slightly less joyous were the attentions of the local fire brigade, who seem to have treated the school as a potential fire hazard. Fire drills always have been a feature of Hornsea life, but when on 2 June, 1971 the Station Fire Officer demanded a drill at 10.30pm on a bitterly cold night, the teacher in charge of the Primary school course then in residence, Mr W.B. Pratt, stoutly resisted, and if the log book is to be believed, appears to have sent the officer packing.

In the days before the M62 and the onset of very heavy traffic, it was possible to cycle to Hornsea from Wakefield, and some boys did so, for pleasure. On 17 September, 1950, for example, while Manygates were staying, 'Depledge cycled from Wakefield to see his pals. He was entertained to tea'. In April 1960, St John's girls' visit was enlivened by a late night call from the Police asking them to accommodate three boys from Snapethorpe who had 'cycled to Hornsea, had no money, and were found cycling without lights at Catwick'. If the boys had intended this to be a romantic assignation with the girls of St John's, they were thwarted, as they were housed in the staff bungalow, given breakfast and seen off the premises by 7.30 the following morning.

Though it is clear that not all visits to Hornsea ran smoothly, perhaps because of the anti-social behaviour of some of the children, or because the weather was unrelentingly dreadful, and though the log books, particularly in the later 1960s and 70s, occasionally betray signs that not all schools planned their stays effectively and so got less out of them, the overwhelming impression that emerges from the records of the visits is one of innocent happiness, and enjoyment of the simple pleasures that Hornsea offered. The sun did shine, if not reliably, and when it did, the Seaside School came into its own. The school field was used for the inter-dormitory sporting competitions, and games of football, rounders, and cricket (and in the Cathedral School's case, a variant called 'Lambert cricket' after Mrs Lambert, the teacher in charge); the children went to the beach for organised games and just to play on the sands; before TV and video began to exercise their sway over teachers and pupils alike, the visitors made their own entertainment in the evenings. In September 1961, it was thought worth noting that TV viewing was still limited to half an hour per evening. The Manygates girls chose to watch *Coronation Street*, described rather cynically by a Snapethorpe teacher in 1966 as 'that exciting programme'. The TV was permitted for special occasions, like the 1966 World Cup, or the return of Sir Francis Chichester from his circumnavigation of the globe the following year. Much effort was expended in planning the end-of-visit concert, especially by the girls' schools, and sometimes committees were formed to plan the other evenings' activities. There was dancing, community sing-songs, charades, quizzes, talent shows, and games. The table tennis set saw heavy use: Roundhill Middle School in 1981 invented their own version, 'table top rounders', played in teams: whoever was batting had to run round the table before hitting the ball again. The girls schools did sometimes favour quieter pastimes: embroidery, needlework and other crafts occupied many an evening. The children went to bed early, fortified with a snack of cocoa with bread and dripping, and often tired out after a day of being out in the fresh air and being kept busy, though even the full programme couldn't always subdue dormitories full of children excited at being away from home.

There was a tradition, at least in some schools, of a Hornsea camp song. It may be that each school had its own version. Certainly, as can be seen from the examples in this book, the tone and content changed over the years. The Cathedral School girls in 1961 are said to have sung the following mock-mournful ditty:

They say that at the Camp School
The boys are very fine.
You ask for Tony Curtis
They give you Frankenstein.
[Chorus]
Oh, I don't want no Hornsea life
Mummy I want to go
Teacher won't let me go
Mummy I want to go home.
They say that at the Camp School
The beds are very fine
But how the heck do they know
They've never slept in mine.

[Chorus]
They say that at the Camp School
The pocket money's fine
They give you 50 shillings
And take back 49.
[Chorus]
They say that at the Camp School
The food is very fine
But what the heck do they know
They've never tasted mine.
[Chorus]

At its best, the Hornsea experience continued to allow, as it did in the first season, staff and pupils to get to know each other as friends, and for the children to enjoy the fun of shared experiences. It was of course not unknown for the girls to develop crushes on the male staff: one girl remembers feigning homesickness to gain the attention of the handsome teacher in charge! The log books can be taken to reflect reasonably accurately the feelings of the visitors. They were not, apparently, read by the Hornsea staff and neither were they seen by 'the office'. Some teachers in charge summed up their visits in a conventionally polite way, but many were happy to be more open in their approval of what Hornsea could offer, and also recognised the contribution the resident staff made to the success of the visits. The matrons and cooks, especially Mrs Paterson, Mrs Nicholson, and Miss Waddell, were instrumental in making Hornsea what it was. 'The welcome of the matron and an excellent meal quickly made the young boys feel at home', recorded Mr A.A. Edwards, teacher in charge of the boys' season from June - October 1954. It was customary for each party to make a small presentation to the staff at the end of the visit. In August 1959, 'the applause for Mrs Nicholson and her colleagues was prolonged and spontaneous'. The Director of one of the music courses noted in April 1968 that 'in expressing our thanks to Mrs

Nicholson and her staff, I find this a pleasure, and not just a duty. Thornes House School referred appreciatively in 1970 to the 'tolerance and good humour of the staff'. The music course leaders seem to have particularly warm relationships with permanent staff at the Seaside School : "they are remarkable, professional people", and Mrs. Nicholson in fact bowed out at a bonfire party at the end of a junior music course in November 1972 :

"Instead of an outing, the children worked hard in their spare time to prepare a bonfire party for the last night. Dead wood was gutted (sic) from the surrounding countryside and the grounds of the Seaside School were cleared up. Even a Summer house was enthusiastically demolished and collected from a helpful neighbour. In addition to the firework and the songs and stories round the fire, Miss Waddell and her staff produced bonfire toffee and parkin cake, and the children roasted chestnuts and potatoes. The presiding genius over this happy evening was Miss Nicholson, whose last night officially in charge of the school this was. The children serenaded her in a ring, carrying their Jack o' Lanterns. A moving occasion, as she has set the tone of this splendid school for over 16 years….."

The Hornsea staff seem to have been adept at producing the sort of food that appealed to young children, and there is scarcely a breath of criticism of the catering, beyond some grumbles about the size of packed lunches : more frequent are the references to the quality and quantity of the meals, "more often than not, children had opportunity for seconds and even thirds". The sense of communal celebration exemplified in the log book entry quoted above is common to many visits, as is the ability of teachers to use Hornsea to impart what would now be known as "personal and social skills". As so often, few teachers sum this up better than Mrs. Cooper, as on the Ings Road/Lawefield Lane visit by 64 girls in July 1959.

….. Hairdressing night. We persuaded many of the girls, whose hair was long and witchlike, to have it cut, and then had a general washing and setting. Fortunately, all three of Ings Road staff are expert hairdressers!

One girl especially had been a big problem, and it was quite an achievement to lop off her locks. The other girls in Hull Dorm., backed up by the staff, and after ….. had had her

hair washed and set, they surprised us all by giving her clothes from their own wardrobes, and taking away her own, which were few and very dirty, and washing them. Even one of the juniors gave her a tube of toothpaste, and somebody else found a hairbrush and some talcum..."

(Mrs Cooper's concern for hairdressing extended to putting out bowls and jugs to catch rainwater, 'past experience having taught me what the hard water here can do to a delicate Wakefield wig'.)

That same visit saw much enjoyment of evening activities. On one evening, the girls had a dance and 'for some curious reason...chose to wear each other's clothes'. On the last night, 'Hull dorm gave a mannequin parade. Hazel Garton was the commère with a superb French accent (really!) and a chic outfit made from a pencil skirt pulled up high and worn as a strapless short dress to show her pretty knees (her own words), also a red towel as a stole and my high heeled shoes. Yvonne Shepherd wore a skirt so tight she nearly died in the attempt to get on the platform modestly... and the rest of us nearly died laughing'.

In 1961, Mrs Cooper noted again that 'the older girls are really good about looking after the little ones. Being away from home seems to bring out the best in them, and it is surprising to see how well they mix...some of the senior girls have shown what fine characters they have, and have been real towers of strength'. She also commented that 'the children...have a very happy relationship with the staff when at the school. From past experience, I know that such relationships stand very firm even when we all return to day school, and I am sure they have lasting value'. The music course director noted also how the older pupils were 'also looking after the social as well as the musical needs of the younger pupils in a most remarkable manner'.

Fancy dress competitions were common features of evening entertainments among the girls schools. Much ingenuity must have gone into the costumes for Cathedral School's party in September 1960, where the winners were Cleopatra (Valerie Field), Cupid (Cathy Colley) and 'spin a disc' (Hazel Cockill). The following party, from Thomas à Becket, also had a fancy dress event which 'caused lots of excitement and made a happy ending to the evening'. When Manygates girls were at Hornsea in September 1964, the winners were Doreen Wells ('my favourite Martian'), Janet Baker ('invisible man') and Christine Bates ('a baby'). The boys schools tended not to go in for such diversions, but they joined in the fun and games as eagerly as did the girls. Joanne Tolson, recalling a visit with Roundhill Middle School in October 1981, thinks that Hornsea had a good effect on the boys in at least one way: 'we were obviously away from home, because even the boys danced at the disco'. And fun was as much the point of Hornsea as more serious teaching, whether it flowed from the Belle Vue bonfire party on 5 November, 1967, fuelled by enormous quantities of food and 10 gallons of sump oil, or the 'hilarious' soccer match played on 11 April 1972 on a music course, where the staff and pupils (of both sexes) who took part were obliged to wear pyjamas and nightgowns and bedroom slippers and plimsolls. The result was a draw. Lawefield Lane in October 1975 found that on the last night that every bed in every dormitory had mysteriously been 'apple pied', and the mystique of the Blue Lady only added to the pleasures of Hornsea, though for Thornes House in April 1974, she only walked once, and turned out to have a beard.

'All the boys said that they have had a very happy time here', was the comment of Mr.Clifton, the teacher in charge of the Manygates visit in July 1948 (he reciprocated the compliment by describing them as a 'grand set of boys'), and this sentiment echoes down the years. Cathedral School girls recorded in 1967: 'the staff and the girls are in full agreement: we couldn't have enjoyed it more!' St. Paul's Alverthorpe in 1971 summed up their Hornsea experience as:

"Good children
Good food
Good weather
Good staff
All add up to a good time"

and in the following year simply commented, 'The children have had a wonderful holiday'.

CHAPTER EIGHT
OUR BENIDORM

It seems so long ago since I last walked into the grounds of Hornsea Seaside School as it was known way back, some thirty two years ago when I spent my two weeks here as a 13 year old. It cost my parents £2 10 shillings to send their little Lupset youth the sixty-six miles with the other hundred lads from Snapethorpe High School.

Across the old East Riding of Yorkshire we sped on the Victoria motor coaches. Only one and a quarter hours and through the trees I spotted Hornsea Mere. On our arrival I was put into Beverley dormitory, second bed on the right. After a good dinner, we were led across the old railway track that Dr Beeching had foolishly axed, then onto the beach. I can still picture the World War Two pill boxes on the beach, about 50 yards out, the eroding cliffs deposited there long ago.

My teacher, Mr John Beardsell, told us we'd two hours to look around before we all met to walk through the little town back to the camp. Great, that gave us time to share our Players No 6 tipped and spend our one shilling and sixpence we were allowed each day. About eight of us paired off and had a go on the Go Karts. On the way back we all spotted two local young girls about our age. We gave them a few wolf whistles but they never even gave us a second look. Their mothers' warning to keep away from those lads from Wakefield worked.

Back for tea of mashed spuds, cabbage, a piece of meat pie followed by ground rice pudding, washed down with as much water as one required. Then it was competition time. Each Dorm had to pick two seven-a-side football teams and battle commenced. After a cool shower it was lights out for 9.30 pm. Nobody slept till well after midnight. Two lads had a fight whilst we "dogged out".

The days passed by quickly. One was spent down at the Mere, four lads to each rowing boat. Once we got out on Yorkshire's largest lake, we all splashed each other till soaked. Mr Beardsell said the Mere was a left over from the Ice Age. Also, I remember a very large pike that was hooked by some lucky angler. It was in a glass case, preserved, or as we said 'stuffed'. Then it was a day at the local Pottery. We watched how the pots were made. I remember the ovens and then into the seconds shop. Every household in Wakefield in those days had a fine piece of Hornsea pottery on its mantelpiece.

Another great day out was Brid. Poor old Pete Larkin had never seen the white cliffs of Flamborough before. Until then he'd never seen the sea, even. Over we all walked in our uniforms to Sowerby Park. Into the large mansion we all went to see the museum of Amy Johnson, a local lass who aviated way back in the pre-war years. Then back to the harbour to eat our packed snaps of cheese sarnies, a rusk-like biscuit and an apple.

The first Sunday morning was spent in the town's church service. Two kids were sent out for whispering. The second Sunday came all the parents. We all went onto the beach and ate fish and chips. My dear mother slipped me two half crowns. Then me Granny gave me a shilling. One kid's dad gave him a ten bob note, jammy sod. We all waved them goodbye and me mam gave me a kiss and all my mates laughed at me. But it didn't matter, cos I loved her. One lad went home because he weed his bed, and was homesick. But he was an only kid, and was rich because his dad had a Ford Anglia.

One night we were all fast asleep when the siren went. It was 2 am. Most of us ignored it till old Piggy Wilson, the Headmaster, came running into the dorm declaring 'the place is on fire'. A great scrum formed around the door, and we all started kicking each other. After he told us spotty youths it was only a practice we all settled back down to the noise of owls hooting and the smell of cigs as Stuart Mountain hung out of a window having a crafty fag.

It was the summer of '66. Every other day all hundred of us lads gathered in the hall around a 20 inch black and white TV to watch England play through the rounds of the World Cup Finals. What a year; England beat the Germans to win at Wembley and I won the School marathon and became Wakefield City champion of 440 yards running, thanks to Berwyn Jones, our PE teacher, who spent many an hour training me. He was our hero; not only did he play on the right-wing for Trinity but also he was picked to represent Great Britain Down Under. He was also an ex-sprinter for GB and was the fastest man ever in Rugby boots. Probably still is.

Then on the 13th I remember all the lads stopping up till midnight. That was the exact time the 'Blue Lady' who haunted this neck of the woods supposedly walked across the

water of the Mere with her head under her arm. I never saw the Ghost lass, but when it went silent, I pulled the covers over my head just in case she happened to pay us a visit. Then one evening at 6.30 pm Pete Cockcroft was given Mr Beardsell's slipper three times across his backside because a dinner lady heard him swear. He was a prefect, and a great kid, hard as nails. I think he's a policeman now.

10am, every morning prompt. 'Right lads, stand by your beds. Inspecting time'. The teacher would walk the full length of each dorm, stopping to look at lads' beds and lockers. 'That's a disgrace lad', he shouted as he pushed all Jack Renold's covers and sheets onto the floor because he had not folded them in a meat sandwich. 'Look at these boy. These boots have not been polished since Monday. Polish them. Ward, you've no hope of getting into the army with boots like that'. David Ward went on to serve two years in the Junior Leaders, and nine years in the Coldstream Guards. Saw action in Northern Ireland. Nice lad. For a full ten minutes the teacher would rub his finger above high ledges, declare 'dust' and 'filth' and then tell us to start all over again. After ten minutes he entered the dorm for the second time and told us 'yours is the dirtiest dorm, so after tea tonight, be ready for a 6.30 pm run to the Mere, you scruffy boys'.

It all seems so long ago, but it was good. A chance to be such mates. It was our Benidorm, our Costa. Carefree days, days I fondly remember. A time of innocence, a time to enjoy team work, honesty. My dear mother spent three weeks at Hornsea Seaside School the very first year it opened in 1938. She too remembers her time here, just before the dark clouds of war came, and the sound of the skylarks gave way to the drone of the Luftwaffe. Forbidden were the next generation of kids to go to Hornsea School for six long years because this coast was a high risk area for an invasion. But thanks to our dads and grandads, Hitler's troops never made it, and the lovely voices of our children can be heard again in our Hornsea School.

Wardens are fair game for everyone. One nameless person was always very enthusiastic when going out for the day, the only problem was he had a slow walking speed of 20 mph, and a fast one of 30 mph. It was our second visit we were aware of this problem and reminded him that we had 10-11 year old children who didn't walk at that speed. The walk from North Landing to the lighthouse proved conclusively that he was either very deaf or had eaten something which disagreed with his intestines. A plan was made. The difficulty of walking at motorway speeds was clearly expressed on the second part of the walk to Bridlington. I had always contended that it was too far to walk so arranged with the driver to pick us up at Sewerby. Being oblivious to our request, the Warden was virtually out of sight within the first few minutes. The shattered tribe of children arrived at Sewerby, boarded the coach and left a message should anyone come looking for a missing school party. A drive to the Sewerby end to Bridlington but no sign of the Warden. He had the pleasure of doing a few extra miles before he finally caught up with the coach.

Every group visiting Hornsea were full of excitement. Whatever you do it is virtually impossible to tire them out, so for the first night few got very much sleep. The second night is different and most teachers express the same sentiments as the teacher who said 'Those little **** will sleep tonight, I'm staying in the dorm until every last one is snoring.' Two hours or so later there was still no sign of this teacher but one had a hell of a row in the dorm. Thinking one was creeping into the dorm quietly, one had just sufficient time to see 20 or so torches switch off. Open the inner door – silence, well nearly, just one prostate teacher snoring away on the floor.

Going to Hornsea was a wonderful time for me. I enjoyed a different kind of life than at home. I did spend some of the school holidays with my gran in Hemsworth but Hornsea was so different. Being the eldest of four girls (later my brother came along) I was often the person to look after my sisters. I'd twin sisters, two years younger than myself, and the youngest one was seven years old. When I wanted to play out, I more often than not had to take one, if not all of them, with me. If I visited friends I sometimes managed to get away on my own. I enjoyed being in the open air, as I lived near a wood I'd often spend a lot of

time in there (something you'd not let children do today).

In the home we had to help with chores like washing up and dusting. Home life was always busy and time away from home and family was valuable time. Sometimes on a Sunday, Dad and a neighbour would round up some of the children from the street and we'd all go for a walk, maybe to Newmiller Dam or even up round Woolley Moor. These trips did not happen often. At other times it would be my friend Pat and me who took the children for walks as we were the eldest two on our street.

Right up to leaving school bedtime was between 7.30 pm and 9 o'clock depending on our ages. So going out to the cinema was not something we did at night time. That was left to Saturday mornings or if we were lucky straight from school.

One of the things that will always stay in my mind about my trips to Hornsea was sitting on a seat outside St Nicholas's Church listening to the juke box playing in a café across the road. It was a typical 50s style café although by the time I went it was into the mid 60s. There was a lot of music about in the 60s but the song that always seemed to be playing was the Honeycombs' *Have I the Right*. Years later my husband and I visited Hornsea and to my surprise the café was still there. It looked as if it had been trapped in a time warp. It looked just the same. I swore if the café had been open for business it would still have been playing the Honeycombs!

There was a night at the cinema when we saw *The Barge* with Harry H Corbett. Later after the film show we had the experience of seeing a live group, The Reverbs. We had visits to Beverley and York and a trip round the Pottery to round off the holiday. I can't say I was glad to leave for home; we stayed for two weeks Friday to Friday with a visit from our family on the second Sunday. Some girls would want to go back home.

On one day we were given a treasure hunt. One clue led us to the park. The park gates were made of wrought iron with every letter of the alphabet on it, with a little poem on it. Although I can't remember it all it did say you could enter as 'your name is wrought on me.' When recently I went back to Hornsea with my husband it was still there, in full it reads, 'Enter Hall Garth with title free, You'll find your name is wrought on me.'

CHAPTER NINE
A FACILITY WELL WORTH PRESERVING

In April 1974, as part of a massive upheaval in local government, Wakefield County Borough ceased to exist, and its responsibilities passed to its successor, the Wakefield Metropolitan District Council. The old Wakefield City authority formed only a relatively small part of new Metropolitan District, which was largely composed of areas formerly part of the West Riding County LEA: and the West Riding officers took most of the top jobs in the new authority. It did not take the new LEA long to decide that the Seaside School needed a fresh sense of direction, and that more use could be made of it as an educational centre, and as a means of providing a social and residential experience for children, for whom this would often be the first time away from home. Hornsea was no longer to be considered as a school; and in 1975 the LEA appointed a Warden to 'make a significant contribution to the development of educational work' at the Centre. The Warden was expected to 'provide a welcoming environment, to offer help, advice and encouragement for children and teachers during their stay…and to take an active part in the teaching both during the daytime and in evening classroom sessions'. He (or she) was also expected to renew contact with local people, to become familiar with the Hornsea area and exploit the possibilities it offered for educational visits and environmental studies; the Warden was now to be resident throughout the year, with breaks in the Summer and at Christmas, when the Centre was closed, and at other times by agreement. This was a significant extension of the 'Teacher in Charge' approach originally adopted for the Seaside School: a permanent appointment was envisaged, with a real opportunity for the Warden to frame the work carried on according to his own interests in environmental studies. The seniority of the post was reflected by the decision to appoint at a Headteacher's salary. Six Wardens have served at Hornsea since reorganisation: Peter Best, Ken Belk, Gordon Jackson, Richard Hall, currently, Jerry Tracey, (whose previous experience had included time at one of the former National Camps Corporation Schools which had passed into LEA management) and Piet Dixon.

The schools which had previously been part of the West Riding system knew little about Hornsea and in some cases, initial impressions were not favourable: South Parade Junior

School from Ossett were surprised at the 'concentration camp design', and Gordon Jackson, later to be instrumental in helping Hornsea survive to its 60th birthday, had similar recollections: 'what a grim place it looked, more like a barrack block from the last war. The two people who introduced us to the Centre endorsed this thinking. The main hall was bleak, austere, very uninspiring, were these two Obergruppenfuhrer and Waffen SS...?', but visitors were quickly won over by the quality of the catering ('the Scots lass...really knew how to feed us') and by the helpfulness and friendliness of the resident staff. 'The wonderful ladies of the kitchen' probably kept the place going in the uncertainties following reorganisation. It did not take long for schools to realise the possibilities the Centre offered 'for a variety of environmental pursuits and studies', and to appreciate how much it 'provides for children a practical lesson in personal and social education in the experience of community living' (which sentiment, expressed in a report to Wakefield Education Committee in July 1990, could just as well have been written in the 1930s, when the idea of the Seaside School was being promoted). The use of the Centre has changed, of course. The idea of two or three weeks stays has long gone: children attend for a week, or sometimes only for a long weekend; and the age range for visitors originally set after 1974 as 7 - 13 gradually contracted to 6 or 7 - 11. The appeal of the visit to Hornsea began to reassert itself. The *Wakefield Express* of 4 August, 1978 carried an article written by Peter Wright, the Chairman of Governors for Walton Junior and Infant Schools, on his experiences accompanying a school visit. He had been a visitor to Hornsea in 1948, while at Cathedral School. He admitted that in his day 'the school was purely for holiday purposes, with very little schooling thrown in, and the object was for every child to enjoy himself', (which might have surprised C L Berry and the other founders of Hornsea), but noted that 'the dormitories were much improved from my childhood days, being bright and well furnished, complete with modern washrooms...compared with the way it was 30 years ago, the modern Hornsea School is like a holiday camp'. Mr Wright's account of his week shows that the traditional Hornsea outings, to the Pottery, Hull Docks, Bridlington and Flamborough Head were still popular, and he drew attention also to a new attraction in

Hornsea town itself - the Museum of Rural Life, which has remained a focus for school visits. His article also shows that there had been some investment in the facilities at the Centre, and this has continued at a modest level to the present day, though it has still not proved possible for the authority to provide covered walkways between the dormitories and the shower block.

By the end of the 1980s, however, the number of children using Hornsea appeared to be declining, and it also seemed that there was a relatively restricted group of schools making regular visits. A questionnaire to schools, circulated by an interested Headteacher, uncovered some dissatisfaction with the way the Centre was being run, and a significant number of respondents indicated an unwillingness to make repeat visits. This may have reflected the rather formal approach to the running of the Centre favoured by the then Warden, which perhaps was a little too redolent of the army camp style of the building for a modern generation of teachers and children. (He recorded his comments on the quality of the visiting schools on the schedule of visits drawn up each year: a large number were characterised as 'bad', or 'rubbish', though a few were given the accolade of 'very good', 'good' or 'not bad'. One school was described as 'good' in spite of there being 'a lot of wet beds'; and on one of the relatively rare holiday period visits, by a group of cubs, there is the doubtless heartfelt comment, 'never again'. Subsequent Wardens tempered their love for Hornsea and care for the site and buildings with a slightly more relaxed attitude to discipline: and usage increased.

To say that Hornsea's affairs had reached a crisis by the end of the 1980s would be an exaggeration, but it was unfortunate that signs of falling use were showing at that time, as changes in the funding of Local Education Authorities meant that its continuation could not be taken for granted. A number of factors coincided to make Hornsea less secure. First, the Education Reform Act of 1988 introduced the concept of 'Local Management of Schools'. Put simply, LEAs were required to delegate the money spent directly on schools, and at least a proportion of the money spent on a range of support, and ancillary, services, to schools themselves, to manage more in line with their own priorities. The finance attaching to facilities like Hornsea was also eligible for delegation : each school would receive its share of the Centre's budget, and it would either decide to spend that share on supporting Hornsea, or use it for other purposes. The LEA decided to use the relatively modest amount of discretion allowed to it to exempt Hornsea from delegation, and to preserve the possibility of access for all schools, but it needed to justify that decision in terms of the wider contribution the Centre made to Education in the Metropolitan District. At the same time, the financial regime to which local authorities were subject was becoming increasingly restrictive, and as budgets tightened, authorities, Wakefield included, came under increasing pressure to protect funding going directly to schools, and to make the cuts required of them in centrally-funded services not regarded as "front line" provision. At one stage, Wakefield supported a number of outdoor and environmental centres: the authority was a member of the consortiums financing Buckden House and the Ingleborough Centre in the Dales, and it maintained a Rural Studies Centre at New Hall Farm, Middlestown. Other curriculum enhancement provision included an Urban Studies Centre and a Drama in Education Service. One by one they fell victim to the increasingly desperate search for savings. The future of Hornsea was discussed in detail by the Education Committee in July 1990, when the then Warden was about to retire. The Centre required a subsidy of about £120,000 per year, and the Chief Education Officer of the day felt constrained to ask the Committee to decide between a number of options, including increasing the charge to children to reduce or eliminate the subsidy: to encourage extra use during holiday periods, by extra district clubs and organisations; to extend and upgrade the accommodation and improve recreational facilities (if capital finance could be found and if the project was seen as a priority); to finance improvements by the sale of land at Hornsea; or to close the Centre and dispose of the site.

The debate on that report made clear how much the members of the Committee valued Hornsea: closure was something they would not contemplate, and a number spoke very strongly about the enjoyment they had gained from their own visits as children, or the value to children in the schools of which they were Governors. They accepted that it might not be

expedient to appoint a permanent Warden until it was possible to be sure that usage could be increased, and they agreed a range of measures to try to reduce the net costs. That decision allowed Gordon Jackson to be appointed Acting Warden; he did much to restore Hornsea's popularity, by 'selling' the Centre to schools uncertain as to whether they should use it, and by communicating his own enthusiasm for what it represented and what it could offer. He introduced a useful extra source of income, by letting the grounds to the Caravan Club for Summer rallies, and was greatly assisted by the willingness of the members of the Hornsea Visiting Sub-Committee (later the Hornsea Panel) to put a degree of pressure on the authority to finance repairs and renewals to the buildings. That the elected members of the authority should take such a clear view of the importance of the Hornsea Centre to Wakefield is testimony to the quality of its work over 60 years. The Hornsea Panel also took a firm stand when in 1997 the LEA was approached by the owners of the Hornsea Pottery, which had by now been enveloped in a 'Freeport shopping centre', with a view to disposing of a strip of land to allow access off the Hull Road to enhance car parking space for extended shopping areas. Though in the end the approach was not pursued, the Panel, like its predecessors, was clear that Hornsea gained much from its spacious surrounds, and that to allow their development would detract from the character of the place. This is an echo of the refusal, forty years earlier, of a request from Hornsea UDC to purchase one or two acres of the southern end of the site for light industrial development, and a similar decision in 1969, when Wimpeys offered to buy some land for housing.

The effectiveness of Jackson's tenure, and that of Richard Hall, a teacher at Lawefield Middle school, both of whom were temporary appointments, meant that by late 1993, the Education Committee felt sufficiently confident about Hornsea's work to sanction an advertisement for a permanent Warden.

Most of the media attention Hornsea has received in its 60 years has been pleasant and supportive. It was therefore distressing that in its Jubilee year, it was to hit the

headlines for the wrong reasons. In June 1998, a number of children from Dane Royd JI school were taken ill on their return from Hornsea and it was discovered that they had been infected by salmonella. A couple of weeks later, some of a group from another school were similarly afflicted. Though the source of the infection was never identified, the Centre was closed prematurely before the end of the Summer term to allow for tests, on the kitchens (which proved negative). Nevertheless, the LEA maintained its view of the long term value of Hornsea and took advantage of the closure to bring forward improvements to the kitchens as well as completing other maintenance work. The Centre re-opened at the end of September, with great success, and under a new Warden, Piet Dixon (whose dog, Straff, a large and benign Alsatian, seemed likely to become a Hornsea character in his own right, and was soon being sent gifts of dog biscuits from his admirers in the schools). Hornsea's future looked bright again. What Hornsea needed to continue to do, and clearly was doing, was to provide the sort of experience enjoyed by The Vale JI school, Knottingley, in September 1997. The Head, in commenting on the visit in a note to the Chief Education Officer, referred to the enthusiasm of the Warden, and his ability to construct a challenging yet entertaining programme for the pupils, the quality of the welcome (and the food) offered by the permanent staff and the opportunity offered by the grounds: 'how (the children) enjoyed the freedom of somewhere safe to run and play - a luxury children rarely find nowadays'. She echoed the views of many of her predecessors when she commented that the staff's 'relationship with the children has deepened, and we all see each of them in a new light', and was positive that Hornsea is 'a facility well worth preserving'.

The activities and routines of The Vale's visit would not be unfamiliar to children attending many years previously. They travelled by coach (Gouldings): during the journey 'hundreds of Love Hearts' were consumed. They were welcomed with a drink and a (home made) biscuit and briefed on the Centre's rules and routines, including a fire drill, shown the 'mystifying art' of making a bed, and told about the daily dormitory inspections.

There was rounders or football on the field, and the customary first evening walk to the beach, using the line of the now disused railway. And on the beach they practised the art of 'skimming' flat pebbles by bouncing them along the surface of the sea. As ever, interesting rocks and stones were collected: how many Wakefield schools have tried to 'strip the beach of its largest rocks'. They finished their first day with a 'Night Walk', designed to get everyone to appreciate the experience of seeing in true darkness - for urban children an awesome experience. That was a less-than-half day's activities. On the Saturday, they got up at 7.30 pm, and tidied the dormitories for inspection, and after a 'hearty breakfast' set out for a long guided walk into the country near the Mere, intended to show off different aspects of the geography, development and flora and fauna of Hornsea, (and allow the collection of interesting feathers) - and as on so many previous visits, also show off the excitement of nature to those who had not known it: on their way back to the Centre, the children (and staff) stood amazed as 'the sky turned dark with hundreds of geese arriving from Siberia for the Winter'. The afternoon was spent at the Hornsea Freeport, getting to know the birds in the 'World of Wings' Centre, exploring Butterfly World, the classic car museum and the adventure playground, and the RSPB Warden at the Mere gave an interesting talk in the early evening. The Saturday night entertainment was a disco, the lineal-descendant of the concerts or talent shows of earlier generations, (this one featured a special performance by 'The Vale Spice Girls'). On the Sunday, the group went to the Leisure Centre, had another tour of the Mere, ate an 'enormous' home-cooked Sunday lunch and caught the coach home. A brief visit, but a full one, with Hornsea doing what it was always intended to: enhancing the school curriculum, giving the children a range of experiences they might not otherwise enjoy, especially the experience of communal living and working as a team; and perhaps, above all, leaving them with 'a collection of wonderful memories'.

CHAPTER TEN
THE STAFF OFTEN HAD A GOOD LAUGH TOO

We took a party of about 30 children to Hornsea in the last week of July 1979. Mr Best, the Warden, was very strict, but the children never grumbled or resented the rules or the discipline. The children had to walk on the footpaths, never run, and were not allowed on the grass as they went from hut to hut. Shoes had to be left at the entrance to the dining room. The children helped to set the tables for meals, clear up afterwards and take turns to help with the washing up. The food was super, well cooked and plenty of it. Grace was said before each meal. Mr Best asked Tracey, a very small girl, to stand up for prayers and she told him she was standing up. We tried not to laugh. The children had to be in bed early. The dormitories had to be kept clean, beds made every morning and lockers tidied. There was a dormitory inspection every morning. A very high standard of tidiness and cleanliness was expected.

We visited Beverley Minster, Hornsea Mere and the beach. Work was done afterwards in the schoolroom, some very good work was produced. The children enjoyed the week very much. It was quite an experience for me. I needed a holiday to recover. It was hard work and a big responsibility but I enjoyed it.

There were highlights aplenty during thirteen years of visiting the Hornsea centre with diverse groups of children from different schools. There were twenty four hours a day on-call duties for seven whole nights, with the wind making violin noises through the slits in the wooden wall alongside your ear during the brief moments of respite on your bunk. There was the time when the party leader said 'everyone stand still, I've lost my contact lens in the sand', and all the eager-to-please youngsters ran to the very spot to help, crushing the lens into the gritty pebbles. Another memory is of detailed plans to have two groups go different ways around a pre-arranged route, meet in the middle and then carry on back to the Centre in opposite directions, and of my leading party of children who gradually, but fairly quickly, realised that I have no sense of direction whatsoever. They had their fears realised when I led them three sides round the same field, which was directly opposite the Centre, led them over the fence and back for tea without losing sight of the starting point.

Then there was the time when a tall gangly lad in a stripey top, saggy trousers, falling-down socks and big boots, carried on walking along the jetty at the Mere until there was no jetty left. The poor lad was up to his middle in cold water, with his unruly red hair sticking up on end, a stricken look on his face, and the whole party in roaring laughter.

Hornsea itself is memorable for the sloping pebbly beach which threatens to suck you into the crashing waves. The suction is so strong that even an adult has difficulty in keeping upright. There are breakwaters at regular intervals which are marvellous places for children to play – dangerous and unpredictable waves crash different heights each side, and there are deep pools around the supporting posts which are hidden by the brownish shade of the water in them. The flotsam on the beach is fascinating in its diversity, from broken shells to driftwood, bricks fallen from the cliffs above, to seaweed of many different shades and slimyness. There is rubbish in abundance – not the normal kind that is left by day trippers, but litter that has been thrown away elsewhere and then travelled by the sea to Hornsea's beach, making it much more attractive, adventurous and interesting. There is usually a variety of types of string, bottles and boulder clay. All sorts of fascinating stones and boulders fall daily from the clay, especially after storms, always making it an interesting place to visit for a spot of beach-combing – a mecca for rock hounds (amateur geologists).

There used to be a little boating pond behind the road on the sea front. Another treat was to pay a couple of pence to hire a boat and try and manoeuvre it around the pond and back to the disembarkation point before you were called in. There used to be some kind of shelter next to the pond, with a floor above from which you could watch for shipping – another source of intense interest. My sister and I once accidentally dropped a flask from the balcony of this building, sending it crashing and smashing to the ground.

Further along the front, there were ice-cream, candy floss and sea-food stalls. Some of these also sold buckets, spades, kites and rock, and would, at moderate cost, fill your flask with tea. We nearly always found it was quite difficult to eat a cornet at Hornsea, because if the wind didn't whip the top off the ice-cream, it would spray it with sand or sea water. It all added to the glory of the day – jam sandwiches with sand, biscuits crunchy with sand, drinks spraying in your face.

Despite the hardships, it was always worth taking a group of children to Hornsea, even if they had had the luxury of a foreign holiday. They always benefited so much from the comradeship and the adventure, the independence and the sharing. The staff often had a good laugh too, eating sweets they would never have eaten at home - blackcurrant and liquorice boiled sweets featured heavily. There were trips to other places which may not be the first choice for many people - Hull Docks, the Marina, the Town Docks Museum, William Wilberforce House and so on. All aspects of the curriculum were covered - pre National Curriculum days, and all enhanced by the first hand experiences that a week away from home was able to offer. Some groups of children were able to mix with children from a different culture for the first time in their lives, while others were made acutely aware that air temperatures can vary from place to place - (Hornsea is ALWAYS cold) - and regretted not listening to the advice to wrap up warmly.

A Note on Sources

Aside from the reminiscences of Hornsea's visitors, the greater part of the material in this book is drawn from the log books kept from June 1948 until March 1974 while the Seaside School was run by Wakefield City LEA. After local government reorganisation, the chore of keeping a log became 'more honoured in the breach than in the observance', and of course the legal obligation to maintain a school log ceased once Hornsea stopped being a school and became an outdoor education centre. After 1974 the log book entries become intermittent, and cease after 1978. If a log was kept for the 1938 and 1939 seasons, and also for the re-opening season in 1947, it has been lost. The detail on the 1938 season is drawn from a specially-published report on the Seaside School's first season produced by the LEA. The log books are deposited in the West Yorkshire Archives, Margaret Street, under the reference WWD4/2/25. The Archives also hold Carl Turnbull's dissertation which he wrote in 1969 as part of his course leading to a teaching qualification. This is particularly helpful as it includes some documentation about how Hornsea was run in the late 1960s which would otherwise not be retrievable. Most of Mr Turnbull's work is a study of individual children at Hornsea and an analysis of their development. I have not used any of this material. The final Archive deposit is a scrapbook which includes much of the press comment, before and after the war, about Hornsea and its aims, some photographs of the opening ceremonies, the 'prospectus' referred to in Chapter Two, the extract from the Holy Trinity parish magazine, which is required reading for all those who can appreciate that particular kind of Church of England roguishness only found in such publications, and other material, on which Chapter Three draws heavily.

The Local Studies collection at Balne Lane Library has sets of Wakefield City Council committee minutes for the period in which Hornsea was first conceived and operated, together with the annual report of the Medical Officer of Health/Principal School Medical Officer, which are especially useful, so far as the historian of the Hornsea Centre is concerned, for the middle to late 1930s. Extensive reference is made to these in Chapters

One - Three, and those Chapters also draw on the Director of Education's Annual Reports from 1934/35 onwards. The custom of writing annual reports of the Director of Education appears to have lapsed after 1938/39, or if it was maintained, the reports were not preserved, and so we do not know directly how C.L. Berry and his successors viewed the success and progress of Hornsea. Committee papers and reports, as opposed to minutes, seem not to have survived, except for those most recently dealt with by the Metropolitan District Council's Education Committee and its Hornsea Visiting Sub-Committee (later the Hornsea Panel).

One or two other references should be acknowledged. The West Riding County Council published a series of reviews of Education in its area, covering the periods 1944 - 54, 1954 - 64 and 1967 - 74. These have useful information about one of Hornsea's contemporaries, Bewerley Park, to which reference is made in Chapter Two. PHJH Gosden and PR Sharp's 'The Development of an Education Service. The West Riding 1889 - 1974' also has some interesting sidelights on outdoor education and open air schooling. Gosden's "Education in the Second World War' contains material on the National Camps Corporation and its schools, and I have drawn on this in Chapter Two. On Hornsea town, I have greatly enjoyed GL Southwell's compilations of archive photographs, which very pleasantly convey a strong sense of place, and the WEA Hornsea local history class, produced in 1993 a publication called *Hornsea a Century Ago*, which although largely dealing with the 1890s nevertheless has much useful material on later years. It is interesting, and salutary, that Mr Southwell's volumes don't include illustrations of the Seaside School, though they do immortalise the holiday home of an organisation called 'The Guild of Brave Poor Things', a charity for long term disabled people, whose title is as redolent of its time as the story of the creation of the Seaside School is of the later 1930s. I hope that this book may be of interest, therefore, not just to Wakefield people, but also in Hornsea itself.

The Balne Lane collection includes some of the old Wakefield County Borough's publications, including *Wakefield Commercially Considered*, to which reference is made in Chapter One, and guides to the City, which give an interesting impression of how Wakefield began to change in the late 1930s. It also, of course, holds a superb collection of local newspapers, on microfilm. The City of Wakefield lacks a narrative history of its development in the twentieth century. My own, admittedly narrow, research for the purposes of this book suggests that there is a fascinating story to tell, and I hope that someone might be moved to write it.